THE DAILY MIRROR OLD CODGERS LITTLE BLACK BOOK NO. 4

THE DAILY MIRROR OLD CODGERS LITTLE BLACK BOOK NO. 4

Edited by
Tony Hoskins and
Fergus Mackenzie

Cartoons by
Nick Baker

MIRROR BOOKS

First published in Great Britain in 1979
by Mirror Books Ltd.,
Athene House, 66/73 Shoe Lane,
London EC4P 4AB
for Mirror Group Newspapers Ltd.
Printed and bound in Great Britain by
Cox & Wyman Ltd., Reading.
ISBN 0 85939 127 2

CONTENTS

COUNTRY MATTERS

WE OLD PAIR are about to indulge ourselves. No, we're not going to pinch Lottie's cheeks, or take a crafty gander at George's pin-up collection. Nothing like that. We are going to take a trip into the country.

For although perforce, we spend most of our lives in town, we get into the open air as often as possible.

Something like seventy-five per cent of the fifty-six million population of Britain live in towns, yet most of us, like the clown who wants to play Hamlet, have a penchant for the country life. We may poke fun at the 'country bumpkin', but we have a sneaking regard for him, a suspicion that he gets a darned sight more out of life than we townies do.

The popularity of the letters from Nellie Mayes, Cornish countrywoman by adoption, and of her own Nature Notebook, is a case in point. So, too, the numerous enquiries we receive on all manner of intriguing country topics.

So now we invite you to join us on a ramble through our collection of rustic pieces. Please remember to shut the gates behind you.

Before setting out, we would like to thank all those kind country folk who have helped us lame city dogs over stiles. For invariably when we have been stumped by some pastoral poser, those good people have supplied us with an answer, straight from the cart horse's mouth, as it were. Sometimes, we suspect, tongue in cheek, and not always scientifically accurate, as we shall see. But always with great good humour, and, accurate or not, wonderfully entertaining.

Poachers ploy

For example, the case of the candle-lit crabs was one which we never really got to the bottom of – were our legs being pulled or not? It started with this letter, from Mrs M. Heath, of Farnham, Surrey:

'Some friends and I stopped at a village pub near the Hampshire coast and an old countryman got into conversation with us. One of his stories intrigued us.

'It concerned an uncle of his who was one of the poaching fraternity back in the days when the gamekeepers came down hard on anyone caught on their preserves with ferret and snares.

'According to this old chap, some poachers dispensed with

these incriminating tools of their trade and used crabs instead! They would go down to the shore and catch a king crab.

'This was harnessed to a long piece of string, a lighted stub of candle was fixed to its back, and it was then pushed down a rabbit burrow whereupon the sight of the perambulating candle made the rabbits bolt, pop-eyed, into nets.

'No salt being available, we fell about laughing, but the old man was very indignant and called upon mine host to verify the story, which he did.

'Strangely enough, another friend heard the same story from a New Forest warden. Is there any truth in it?'

We Old Pair sat on the fence, having long since learned not to scoff at such stories. To us, the phrase 'rustic simplicity' is a contradiction in terms. For, as we told Mrs Heath, there's nowt so crafty as a country yokel after a rabbit – or a pint!

Yokel joke

However, some readers had no doubts that Mrs Heath was being taken for a ride. Like Leslie Rawlings, of Dereham, Norfolk:

'The crab and candle story is a well-known countryman's leg-pull. The 'furriners' from town look down on countrymen as ignorant yokels. They know it, so they back each other up with these stories.

'I'm touching seventy-two and have snared and ferreted hundreds of rabbits. The only way to bolt a rabbit is with a ferret.'

And Mrs I. Wright, of Brookhill, Sheffield:

'My late father, an old sea dog, used to tell this story, with the rider that if the crab were used regularly by the same poacher, it could be trained to use its big claw to snuff the candle when back at the surface!'

But Mr G. Golding, of Great Bedwyn, Wilts, was equally emphatic that the story was genuine:

'The use of crabs to bolt rabbits is certainly authentic and was practised along much of the South Coast, certainly in Kent where I used it successfully as a boy thirty to forty years ago. The theory is that the crab will keep crawling to get away from the light of the candle, and the rabbit bolts for the same reason. And of course it's cheaper and easier to catch a crab than to keep a ferret.'

Deadly methods

Mr F. Hollands, of Chester, certainly sounded as if he knew what he was talking about:

'Crabs were indeed used for catching rabbits. It was known as 'night-lighting' for night-lights, not candles, were used. Here are some other tricks used by poachers.

'"Burrow stuffing" was the art of rabbit catching by preventing their return into their burrow by making the holes "blind".

'"Bird wooing" was the art of obtaining roosting pheasants by burning sulphur at the base of their roosts. Of course, it had to be a windless night. This was sometimes known as "Manna from heaven".

'And "pheasant hooding" was the art of placing the old-fashioned triangular sweet bag into a pre-dibbed hole near a pheasantry. A couple of raisins were put in the bag, some bird lime smeared round the neck of the bag, then all that was needed was a club.'

No doubt all those methods were horribly effective and Mr Holland's letter serves to show that poaching is a matter of deadly – and often cruel – earnest as far as the prey is concerned. Nevertheless, to most folk, town or country, the poacher remains a romantic figure, except, of course, to landowners and gamekeepers.

Fair gamekeeper

But there are poachers and poachers, as this letter, published some years ago, testifies. Mr W. S. Whales, of Arminghall Manor Estate, near Norwich, wrote:

'Speaking as a gamekeeper and a countryman who loves the countryside, I would like to put on record my disgust at the "poachers" of today – a greater menace to the countryside than any litter-bug.

'They work in gangs. They use motor cars. And by the light of their headlamps, they shoot at anything that flies or runs. I often wonder what a real poacher of pre-war days would have had to say about their carryings-on.

'The real poacher knew what to kill and what not to kill. He only took the game he was after. He knew how to use the gun, trap, snare, net – and his dog. And knew *when* to use 'em too.

'The poacher's lurcher – a cross twixt greyhound and

sheepdog trained from a pup – would round a field and bring hares and rabbits to a net as easily as kissing your hand. And he'd be back at his master's side in a trice when he knew a gamekeeper was about.

'And he wasn't the poacher's only ally. He was alerted by a blackbird's sudden twittering, or when a nightjar stopped whirring, or a jay shrieked. Yes – the poacher knew his friends and respected them.

'What a difference between today's gangs who blunder into the hedgerows and that real "professional" of days gone by!'

Mr Whales's letter produced an interesting response from one of those 'real professionals' who, understandably, wished to be known simply as R.S.:

'My father first took me poaching at five years old and I am now thirty, so I have seen the same changes as the gamekeeper who wrote in your column. I fully agree with him.

'I've even got to the stage when I stand in the pub next to the gamekeepers and landowners admitting I'm a poacher and offering to help keep these other motorised so-called poachers off their land. Some may call me a turncoat, but no, I am just a respecter of nature.'

Sinner or saint?

A poacher's wife, writing anonymously from Finchampstead, chimed in with this defence of her husband's profession:

'Critics of poachers should remember the proverb of the true poacher: "He who takes the game from the land is a thief and a poacher; but he who takes the land from the game becomes a lord or a squire".

'The poacher is the salt of the earth. He saves the parish councillors the job of walking the public footpaths kicking down fencing which bad landlords put up to stop people enjoying the beautiful countryside.

'He is always handy to help put out a forest fire and help cattle caught on barbed wire fencing.

'The landowner may curse him, the magistrate fine him, and the public may misunderstand him, but many people know and bless the poacher.'

We still reckoned the game would take some convincing!

Twelve for the pot

But we could be in no doubt at all that every poacher has a heart of gold after reading this account of a wartime Christmas. It was told to us by another lady who wished to be nameless:

'This particular Christmas we had no meat at all and mother was worried. There were twelve homes in all, near at hand, and all were in the same plight. "Never mind," said father, "Tom and I won't let you down."

'It was pouring with rain, but, undaunted, off they went on their bikes to find out which of the two village pubs the gamekeeper was drinking in. Having refreshed themselves, they headed in the opposite direction and, as only countrymen know how, commenced to look for their quarry.

'It was well after midnight when the door opened and my father stood there, soaked to the skin, but not a bird in sight.

'"Sorry, mate," he said, "it will mean bread and jam this year."

'"Where is Tom?," my mother asked, and out of the darkness, soaking wet, with a sprig of holly on top of his head, grinning from ear to ear, came Tom with a garland of twelve birds around his neck!

'"A pheasant Christmas to you, Margaret," was all he said.'

'Tis his delight . . .

A reader who described herself as 'A poaching widow' pointed out the snags of the business:

'My husband works on the buildings all summer and is as good as gold. But directly the autumn is upon us, the woods "call" him not only by day but by night as well – with disastrous results if he is caught.'

Presumably, being a part-timer, her husband didn't know one of the tricks of the trade which was the subject of this account of the feat of a local poacher overheard in a Sussex pub by a reader on holiday there:

'An eye-witness described how he had just been talking to the poacher in a spinney, through which was flowing a pretty fast stream, when a gamekeeper suddenly appeared.

'It seemed certain that the poacher was going to be caught red-handed. But when this eye-witness turned he was flabbergasted to see that the poacher had vanished. The gamekeeper went on his way, never suspecting that he was passing within three feet of a poacher.

'The poacher had obeyed the cardinal rule by which all of his kind survive – namely, never be seen. He had submerged himself completely in the river and stayed under until the danger had passed.'

Two-legged foxes

Mention of that cardinal rule reminds us of those famous Hertfordshire poachers, the Fox twins of Stevenage, whose own father did not even know them apart.

The Fox boys – Ebenezer Albert and Albert Ebenezer – learned to exploit their identical appearances as highly successful poachers, always using each other's names whenever caught and thus establishing alibis.

They had eyes like cats, and when shooting at night they reputedly used a damped wax-vesta match on their foresights – moistened so that the phosphorus in the match head became luminous. Ebenezer Albert claimed a record of eight pheasants with one barrel, and a bag of 1,000 rabbits a month.

The Foxes were immortalised by a pub in Stevenage New Town, 'The Twin Foxes', which has a two-faced sign, one face showing the silhouettes of the Fox twins, cloth-capped and carrying shotguns, the other showing the masks of twin foxes. Can any poachers have been more aptly named?

No fleas on Reynard

For the fox is the supreme poacher of the animal kingdom. His cunning at stealing pheasants, getting into hen coops, and evading capture are legendary. But is Reynard as super-intelligent as his reputation suggests?

Ramsgate, Kent, reader, Mr G. Weller, was told by a farmer friend that when a fox wants to rid himself of fleas, it will go into a pond backwards, slowly submerging from the tail upwards. The idea, according to the farmer, is that the fleas run up the fox's body to its head, then the fox simply ducks its head under and swims to the bank, a flealess fox. 'But,' said Mr Weller, 'the farmer knows I'm a Londoner so I think he is kidding me.'

We sympathised, for we had heard a similar story and had

never been sure whether to believe it or not. In the version we heard, the fox was supposed to be even craftier in that he went into a river holding a piece of rabbit fur in his teeth and when the fleas migrated from him to the rabbit fur, he simply let it go, carrying his erstwhile boarders downstream.

Somehow we couldn't quite believe that Reynard's powers of reasoning were that acute. Having said as much, we were accused by several readers of underestimating the animal. Eric Dymond, of St Day, Redruth, Cornwall, was one who could only believe the evidence of his own eyes:

'Years ago, when I was a boy, I was standing at my bedroom window getting dressed for school, when I noticed a fox enter a nearby pond, holding what appeared to be a piece of sacking in its mouth.

'It swam out a short distance, completely submerged, then swam back, leaving what it had been carrying floating on the water.

'I went out immediately to see what the fox had left and it turned out to be a bunch of dry grass – which was absolutely alive with fleas! I am not joking.'

Wash and brush up

Likewise from Mr J. Mansey, of Dorking, Surrey:

'During the First World War, I was assisting old Besty – Mr Best, a shepherd – to dip a flock of sheep. We had prepared the dip when Besty suddenly said: "Look at that vixen, boy, by Clay Copse". There was a vixen ambling along, picking sheep's wool off the bramble bushes. "Keep still," Besty whispered, "You may never again see what she's up to." The vixen went to the dip and slowly waded in until only her nose was sticking out of the water. Besty and I went on removing the ticks from the sheep before dipping them. Then he said: "See if she's still in the dip – if not, look at the wool floating by the stop."

'The vixen had gone, but the wool was a mass of fleas.'

Fifteen-pint fox

Mr C. Jackman, of Ripley, Surrey, had good cause to remember a similar childhood incident:

'As a boy, more than seventy years ago, I lived in a cottage with a garden which reached down to the Wey Navigation

Canal. One day I was fishing for tiddlers when my father came down with his muzzle-loading gun. "Sit still," he said, "There's a fox in the canal, flea-cleaning." When it got out on the tow path, he shot it. As he went over the bridge to get it he told me: "Now you can catch fish as fast as you can." Sure enough, within a short time I had between twenty and thirty dace and gudgeon that were feeding on the fleas.

"Father skinned the fox and walked six miles, there and back, to sell it for 2s 6d, which was good money then and bought him fifteen pints of beer.'

Fortunately for the fox in this next account, the story-teller's Dad wasn't bothered about beer money!

Jack Wright, of Ingatestone, Essex, recalls:

'When I was nine or ten – I am now eighty-three – I went with my father one Sunday morning shooting pigeons off a pea field. He had built a hide with branches under an old oak tree near a pond, the pigeons coming to the tree, then down to the pond.

'Suddenly father whispered: "Look Jack, a fox." It came to the pond carrying a stick, walked into the water, swam around two or three times, got out, dropped the stick, shook himself and trotted off. My father would have shot it, but the skins were not worth anything those days. Now they fetch £18 each. What a difference!'

Natural mistake?

Similar eye-witness reports from various parts of the country seemed to clinch the argument. But, while not doubting their sincerity, could it be that those untrained observers had jumped to their own – wrong – conclusions?

Ted Bartlett, of Send, Surrey, certainly thought this was the case:

'As a field naturalist who has studied both the badger and the fox for more than forty years, I have been interested in the letters about foxes walking into water with a mouthful of dried grass or fur to rid themselves of fleas.

'Seeing a fox behaving thus, even good countrymen have assumed that the animal is de-fleaing itself, but this is a misinterpretation of what is really happening.

'True, foxes have been seen swimming with grass or fur in their mouths, but the material around the jaws is merely the result of the fox's seizing mice or voles in the grass or digging a baby rabbit from a nest – it grabs grass and all.

'As soon as the prey is dead, the fleas on the prey leave the body and infest the grass. So it is the prey's fleas, not the fox's, which are found floating.

'Further, it is not possible for a fox to wash out its own fleas in this way. For its fleas live in the close, soft hairs next to the skin, which remain dry even when the fox is immersed.

'Even if the undercoat did become waterlogged, the fleas would be helpless to move about.'

Foe or friend!

Bert Henri, of Treasure Holt Farm, Great Clacton, Essex, agreed, adding:

'I have made friends with many wild foxes and have never yet found any with fleas on them. The fox, contrary to what the bloodthirsty hunting fraternity tell us, is a friendly, clean animal, more intelligent than a dog and more affectionate than a cat, when you get to know it. I have had one vixen coming here since 1973. She has raised several families, the cubs leaving in the autumn.

'Foxes are useful to have around as they keep down rabbits, rats and mice and other vermin.'

Mr Henri also sent us photos of his own dog and kitten playing with a vixen which was obviously intelligent enough to know a foxophile when it met one!

Bird charmer

Before leaving the subject of foxes, here is another trick they are supposed to use. It was told to us by Dick Rushton, of East Grinstead, W. Sussex:

'Pheasants usually roost on the lower branches of trees and, providing there is sufficient light, a fox will position himself below a bird, then start walking from side to side. The pheasant, watching from above, moves its head from side to side, becomes giddy, falls from its perch – and the fox gets the bird.

'I have no proof of this, but the old folks in Berkshire, where I was born nearly seventy years ago, believed it.'

Other readers claimed to have witnessed foxes thus charming birds off trees, though most said that the animal gave its prey vertigo not by walking from side to side but by running round and round the tree.

Pheasant surprise

Pheasants may be bird-brained enough to fall for a trick like that, but they apparently have one uncanny knack of their own which country folk turned to good use. We found out about it by chance when Mrs Margaret Rowe, of Truro, Cornwall, made this curious observation:

'Every night, at 9.05, a pheasant nearby calls, and my brother says that it is a sure sign that Concorde is approaching.

'We have to admit that soon after we do hear the booms of Concorde, but can there really be a connection?'

We joked that possibly the pheasant mistakes Concorde for a supersonic shotgun, but there was more to it than we imagined. First, Mr A. Pears, of Brent Knoll, Somerset, wrote:

'I can well believe that a pheasant could give early warning of the approach of Concorde. During the war we lived at Solihull, near Birmingham and, sure enough, a few minutes after George, our pet pheasant, called and showed signs of agitation, the sirens would sound. Then we would hear the throb of enemy aircraft passing over to bomb the city, or the Spitfire factory at Castle Bromwich.'

Zep spotters

And Mrs A. Sparrow, of Rickmansworth, Herts, confirmed:

'During the First World War we lived in Norfolk and a man on a bike used to ride out from the Post Office to warn us of impending air raids, there being no sirens in those days. My father told him: 'Don't bother to come and warn us – the pheasants on the estate three miles away always warn us.'

'And they did – they rose, as one, in their hundreds, and could be heard for miles. Then we would see the Zeppelins come over.

'I think they were looking for the royal house at Sandringham, for they dropped a bomb on a local village church.'

We reckoned it must have been a field day for the local poachers when those Zeps came over the coverts! Then we made one of those happy discoveries called serendipity.

Timeless observation

We bought a second-hand copy of *Wildlife in a Southern County* by that most delightful of country writers, Richard Jefferies, and in it we found this passage:

'The pheasants that wander away from the preserves and covers up under the hills far down in the meadows as the acorns ripen, roost at night here in the copse; and should a storm arise, after every flash of lightning gleaming over the downs the cocks among them crow. So, too, in the daytime, after every distant mutter of thunder the pheasant cocks crow in the preserves, and some declare they can see the flash, even though invisible to human eyes, at noonday.'

Jefferies wrote that in 1878 and it pleases us to think that, no matter how drastically his countryside has changed in the century between, some of the things, at least, about which he wrote so lovingly remain unaltered in these Concorde days.

Fowl influence

The fox's trick of mesmerising pheasants, mentioned by Mr Rushton, reminds us of a similar country topic on which we had a huge mailbag – the art of hypnotising hens. Mr L. Froom, of Redcar, Cleveland, asked us to confirm a trick he had performed as a lad which involved chalking a white line on the floor, and placing a hen's beak on the line, whereupon the bird remained motionless as if glued to the line. Mr Froom's workmate refused to believe him – but scores of other readers put pen to paper to verify his story. Like Mr T. Scarth, of Crayford, Kent:

'As a boy, I worked on a farm and performed that trick many times. Another feat was to hold a hen on its back and to slowly wave my hand to and fro before its eyes. After a few moments the hen could be released, but it would lie perfectly still until I snapped my fingers.'

And the aptly named Mr R. Birdseye, of London N5:

'When I was with the Army in India, each member of the regiment was given a live chicken to fatten for our Christmas dinner. We used to get about ten out of a crate and put their beaks on the floor and draw a line from the beak, about two feet. We could then leave them, picking them up later.'

Mr R. Bullock, of Goldthorpe, S. Yorks, told us that he, too, was a disbeliever, until a workmate offered to demonstrate:

'Having chalked a straight line about five yards long down the garden path, he proceeded to place the hens one by one on alternate sides, heads down, along the line. The birds stayed motionless in that position for several minutes, after which they sauntered off in their own good time.'

Cock-eyed

By now, we were as mesmerised as the chickens, but variations on the theme continued to pour in. Mr I. Snook, of Whitchurch, Cardiff, pointed out:

'The same effect could be achieved by tucking the hen's head under its wing and spinning it round three times. I tried the latter method when I visited a farm, catching each hen in turn, ending up with about a dozen hens all fast asleep in a row.

'I then caught a cockerel and held its beak to the ground. Having no chalk, I simply picked up a stick and drew it sharply away from the cock's beak. He stayed there, so I caught another cockerel, placed him at the other end of the row and did likewise. I was amazed at my efforts, with a cock at each end and a dozen hens between, all in a deep state of mesmerism!'

Mr G. Johnson, of Teffont Magna, Salisbury, recalled:

'During the last war, in Burma, we were often short of a meal, so hypnotised the native chickens by drawing a line on the ground. The villagers, thinking we had put the evil eye on their fowls, used to give us eggs to remove the spell!'

And Mr J. Haworth, of Accrington, Lancs, reminded us:

'This trick was done in the film *Adventure*, starring Clark Gable and Greer Garson.

'The only difference was that Clark Gable just made a line in the dust with his finger and placed the hen's beak in the furrow. The hen stayed motionless.'

Mule trainer

Finally, Iva Maer, of Bridgwater, Somerset, asked us:

'Did you know that mules were also susceptible to the hypnotic effect of a white line – probably one of the best-kept secrets of the Second World War! This trick was used when large numbers of these animals were being unloaded from ships or gliders.

'Once the white line had been drawn around them, they could be left totally unattended until required. And only when they heard the magical words "Whooday, whooday", would the reluctant mules budge outside their circle.

'Some blokes thought it was partly due to the fact that mules see in three dimensions and the white line therefore represented a thick white wall to them.

'But whatever the reason, as every Chindit will gratefully recall, on certain operations those animals could be left for several days safe and sound within their white circle.'

We Old Pair hadn't realised that mules were as thick as *that*, but then our silly ass George often goes round in small circles for days!

Cock and hen story

It was another chicken question which confirmed an old suspicion of ours – that 'experts' don't know it all. Teresa Potter, of Bradwell-on-sea, Essex, wanted us to convince sceptical friends that there is such a thing as a crowing hen, that is, a hen which has turned into a cock.

We were inclined to agree with Teresa, but poultry experts we consulted told us that hens do not change sex. They suggested that the crowing 'hens' were, in fact, cockerels all the time, but were wrongly sexed in the first place.

In the event, it seemed we had consulted the wrong experts in the first place! Our subsequent mailbag contained dozens of accounts of sex-change chickens.

Mr E. Troth, of Sidemoor, Worcs, reported:

'My mother-in-law had eight hens – three White Leghorns, two Rhode Island Reds and three black ones. Now, one of the Whites did everything that a cockerel should do, "treading" all the others, and calling them for food before she herself would eat, and getting up on a box to crow just like a real cockerel.

'Yet she had definitely not been wrongly sexed for, with great difficulty and much groaning, I will admit, she would lay a lovely large egg.'

Mr R. Hall, of Loose, Kent, gave this account of the phenomenon:

'When I was twelve I was given a hen bantam. In its first laying year it laid more than a hundred eggs. The second year it didn't do nearly so well. I noticed that its comb grew, then one morning I found it sitting on top of a 14ft high barn door, crowing.

'Since then I have owned four crowing hens. They were all birds between two and three years old. They even developed spurs. When crowing, the sound is exactly like that of a young cock – they cannot hang on to the last note like that of a well-developed cock.

'They are still capable of laying, but produce so few eggs that they don't earn their keep. I doubt if a modern poultry keeper would come across one, because hens are now usually killed off after one year.'

Which seemed to prove at least half of the old proverb:

'A whistling maid and a crowing hen, are neither fit for God nor men.'

Bemused Bantam

But down on Hope's Grove Farm, Tenterden, Kent, things appeared to be even more cock-eyed. Mrs M. Hankinson explained:

'On this farm the boot seems to be on the other foot. Our Rhode Island bantam cock, Mr Cocky, sometimes thinks he is a hen!

'The children have been greatly amused to see him fashion a nest from hay and straw and then proceed to sit for hours as if to lay an egg. From time to time he peers underneath to see if an egg has arrived, but of course it never has.

'In other respects he is quite normal. He crows loudly at daybreak and is the father of several chicks – hatched from eggs laid by his wives.'

We reckoned if Mr Cocky ever did get to the point of lay, it would fair make his comb stand on end!

Back to normal

We were grateful to Mr A. Tiffen, of London E17, for an explanation:

'The Poultry Association of Great Britain has researched into the phenomenon of cock-hens as they are known. They found that hens can assume the characteristics of cocks due to certain hormone imbalances.

'A certain hen laid eggs in its first year, then assumed the appearance of a male and crowed strongly for its second year. Then it moulted back to the normal plumage of a hen and resumed laying.'

Animal magic

Very few farmers, or farm-workers, we Old Pair have met have been sentimental about their animals. Which isn't surprising, for they could hardly afford to be when their own livelihood is at stake. But the sensible ones, at least, treat their stock humanely, if only for practical reasons. However, stories are told of certain characters who have an affinity with animals and have achieved Dr Dolittle's dream of being able to 'talk to the animals'.

Possibly the best example are those mysterious people known as 'horse whisperers'. We had heard of them vaguely, but we learned more about them after we published this letter, from Bernard Horisk, of Garvaghey, Co. Tyrone:

'In this locality there is a rumour (or is it a legend?) about certain people known as "whisperers" who could enter the stable of a vicious horse and, after a period behind closed doors, emerge with a docile and obedient animal.

'It is said that a dangerous horse belonging to the late Queen Victoria was transformed into a valuable animal by one of these people. Do you know anything about this practice?'

We told Bernard that George Borrow, the 19th century writer who spent much of his life among gipsies, wrote of 'one who is an expert whisperer and horse sorcerer' in his book *The Bible in Spain*. And in *The Romany Rye* he referred to the gipsy trick of 'whispering' horses out of fields and the use of certain words by Irish gipsies to enrage or calm horses.

Horseman's word

Herbert Imlah, of West Didsbury, Manchester, then informed us that he had witnessed a horse whisperer at work more than fifty years ago in his native north of Scotland:

'A massive Clydesdale stallion required the vet's attention to a sore on a hind leg. The gear to keep the horse under control – a sling with block and tackle over the stable rafters – was all ready, and the vet was preparing his implements, when Jake came in.

'Many people thought Jake was somewhat simple, but he had the "Horseman's Word" and so was highly respected by the fraternity to which all true horsemen belonged. "You'll nae need a' that gear," said Jake. And, after a short conversation, the vet was sufficiently convinced to do some preliminary probing while Jake held the horse's head and murmured gently.

'Eventually the entire operation was completed, including stitching and dressing, and in all that time the great horse stood like a rock, apart from the occasional muscular quiver.

'As a mere lad, I was fascinated by the effect Jake had on that animal.'

Bone of toad . . .

Obviously Jake didn't divulge the secret of his strange powers, but Bob, who asked us not to print his name or address, threw a little more light on the subject:

'The classic example of "whispering" confidence into a horse in racing circles concerned the Queen's horse Aureole, which finished second in the 1953 Derby. Aureole came under "treatment" from an alleged Harley Street specialist who would stand in its box at Captain Boyd-Rochfort's stable at Freemason Lodge, Newmarket, and think calming thoughts at it.

'But this business of "whispering" is extremely ancient. Potent "magic" was made by "horse witches", using a certain bone from the natterjack toad. Having killed your toad, you had to leave it in a whitethorn bush for 24 hours, bury it in an ant hill for a month, then take it to a stream at full moon.

'You then watched as the bone – a forked bone, probably part of the pelvis – detached itself from the skeleton and floated upstream! Then you baked it, crushed it and mixed it with a little oil. To control your horse, you wiped his tongue, nostrils, chin and chest with it. Or maybe you kept the bone whole under your armpit and just touched the horse with it. And some "witches" simply breathed into the horse's nostrils.

'But the basis of all this was the same – the utilisation of the horse's acute sense of smell. It wasn't the powdered toad's bone which made the horse do what its master wished. It was the sweet aromatic oil with which it was mixed, or the familiar body smell of a kind master transmitted by the bone, or again the sweet smell of his breath.'

A rareyfied gift!

Then Richard Morris, of Blackwood, Gwent, referred us to another book:

'The "whispering" treatment used to control horses is described in an old book, *Every Man His Own Farrier*, by Francis Clater. It was published by Milner and Co., London.

'One section deals with a visit to Britain in 1857 by a Mr Rarey, whose command of the secret, spell-binding language was such that he aroused the astonishment of all who observed him, from the Royal Family to provincial horsemen.

'His technique was to show extreme kindness towards the animal, convincing him that man is his natural master and friend. He could, within a quarter of an hour, gain the confidence of the most unruly horse.

'On one occasion, he tamed a handsome bay charger, belonging to the Prince Consort, to the extent that he could jump on its back, flourish an umbrella, and beat a tattoo on a drum, while the animal stood motionless.

'Mr Rarey came from Ohio and was the son of a horsebreeder.'

No foaling

We were obliged to Wilfred Wallace, of Great Barton, Suffolk, for another piece of horse sense we'd not heard before:

'Your recent letters on horse lore remind me of the time I was talking with a retired farm horseman and remarked on a saffron shrub in his garden. "Ah," said old Bill, "whenever I've moved I've allus took that bush with me, and now that hosses are a thing o' the past, there's no harm in tellin' yew what us hoss chaps used it for. Say you got a good working mare in your stable and the gaffer want her in foal and yew don't. What yew do is take a few dried leaves o' that saffron and mix it up in her bait when yew knows the stallion is due ter call and your mare'll never click for a foal."'

We couldn't help wondering if that crafty bit of contraception worked on the dairymaids, too!

When bees are bereaved

A further example of humans communicating with the animal – or in this case, insect – kingdom is the old custom, still followed by many beekeepers, of 'telling the bees' when there is a death in the beekeeper's family. Failure to take this precaution is thought to lead to the swarm itself dying or deserting the hive.

A remarkable instance of this was reported to us, years ago, by a Surrey reader. She wrote:

'An old gentleman we knew kept bees for years. He gave one hive of bees to his neighbour although the hive remained in the old chap's garden.

'Early last month the old gentleman was found dead. The next morning a relative went to look at his bees and found that they were all dead – except those in the hive that happened to have been given to the neighbour. Have you Old Pair ever heard of anything like this before?'

Naturally, we told her about the old belief, mentioned above, but in this case we think there was a logical explanation. In the autumn bees should be given a feed of sugar and syrup to tide them over the winter. The old chap died in the January and it may be that he had not previously fed his bees and consequently they died from starvation some time before their owner's death.

Swarm work

There may be no logical explanation for this next ritual practised by apiarists but, like many of the old country ways, it would appear to be effective. The subject was introduced by Mr F. B. Green, of Southall, Middlesex.

'When I was a small lad (fifty-five years ago) I lived with an uncle who was a keen beekeeper. One of my jobs, when bees were about to swarm, was to stand by the hive and bang a piece of metal.

'I was told that this would prevent the queen bee heading off into the distance, taking her swarm with her. However, it didn't always seem to work, and I often had to chase after them for miles over ploughed fields.

'Have you heard of this custom, and is there anything in it?'

An authority on bees told us that banging on metal has no

effect whatsoever on swarms, and beekeeper Stan Smith, of Ipswich, Suffolk, agreed:

'The custom of "tanging of the bees" to induce a swarm to settle has persisted over the years for a number of reasons, most of them now discredited.

'One, it was felt that the great noise of "tanging" tins would interfere with the bees' ability to communicate with each other and so unsettle them.

'Again, bees will return to their hives when thunder indicates rain is on its way, so it was thought a banging noise would have a similar effect.

'More realistically, while it was still the law that a beekeeper could follow his swarming bees wherever they went, on to any property, the loud banging alerts all and sundry that Bill Blogg's bees are swarming and he is in full pursuit to reclaim them.'

Grandma tanged 'em home

However, a number of apiarists insisted to us that 'tanging' was not merely a bee in their bonnets but really does make the bees behive themselves. Bee that as it may, William Clabburn, of Grays, Essex, had a delightful memory of a practical demonstration:

'I was brought up by my grandparents in a remote Norfolk village. Grandma kept bees and I twice saw her "tanging" a swarm, or "ringing 'em home" as she called it.

'On the first occasion the swarm had settled in a huge cherry tree in the postmistress's orchard. The branch was too fragile for a ladder, so I was sent back to our cottage to fetch a large iron frying pan.

'Grandma then picked up a stone and began to beat a rhythmic tattoo on the pan. After a minute or two the swarm broke away from the tree where it had been hanging like a rugby ball, and circled above us.

'Granny slowly walked back to the cottage, some 400 yards, the swarm circling above her while we onlookers followed at a safe distance, scarcely able to believe our eyes.'

Seeing is believing, whatever the experts say!

Nature's nasties

Two of the less attractive creatures of the countryside but

which nevertheless seem to fascinate townies are the snake and the rat.

Only three species of snake are found in Britain, the grass snake, the smooth snake and the adder. Unfortunately, most people – even country folk – have an inordinate fear of any snake and all three are often killed on sight.

Yet neither the grass nor the smooth snake are venomous, though the smooth may try to bite if handled. And the adder, though poisonous, will not willingly attack humans, preferring to glide away unless it is actually touched. Deaths from snake bite are very rare in this country – there are far more fatalities from wasp stings.

It is not easy to distinguish the smooth snake from the adder, because both have colour variations and the smooth sometimes has a V mark on its back, as does the adder. The smooth snake is also rarer, being found only locally in southern England, so it is safer to assume that if it looks like an adder it is!

The grass snake also varies in colour, anything from greenish-brown to black, but is easily identified by a yellowish-white collar round the nape of the neck.

Snakes alive

A curious thing about the smooth snake is that it is ovoviviparous, that is, it lays eggs which then hatch immediately, the young, about eight inches long, being active instantly.

The grass snake, on the other hand, lays eggs in warm places such as manure or compost heaps and the young hatch out in some six to ten weeks.

The adder is viviparous, giving birth to anything from six to twenty live young. We believe it may well be this fact which gave rise to an old country belief that an adder when cornered with its young will swallow them for safety. A famous zoologist once offered a reward to anyone who could prove this theory, but it seems likely to us that the belief arose from pregnant adders being killed and being then found to contain their unborn offspring.

Adder worried

Mrs Irene Wallace, of Harlow, Essex, raised another ancient adder question when she asked us:

'Can you tell me if adders are deaf? I have lived in the country all my life but I'm not sure, though there is an old saying about the adder:

If I could hear as well as see
No one on earth would pass by me.

'I would appreciate an early answer, because there are a number of adders in this district!'

We advised her in that case to keep her wellies on! Adders were long thought to be deaf – in Psalm 58 there is a reference to 'the deaf adder that stoppeth her ear' – because they have no external ear. But they do have an internal 'ear' which receives sound vibrations through the body.

However, the sight and hearing of snakes as a whole are poor, their sense of smell and touch being far more important.

How rats poach eggs

Dick Rushton, the East Grinstead reader referred to earlier who first raised the question of foxes mesmerising pheasants, also sparked off an interesting series on rats when he mentioned their trick of stealing chickens' eggs.

According to Dick, two or more rats work together, one lying on its back so that the others can roll an egg into its upturned paws. The first rat is then towed away, egg and all, by its tail.

Again, we old Doubting Thomases took the story with a pinch of salt only to have it verified by numerous other readers. Mr W. Cruttenden, of Ore, Sussex, though, thought Dick hadn't got it quite right:

'True, one rat lays on its back and gets the egg in its paws, but the second rat doesn't pull the first by its tail because this would rough up the hairs and make it hard to pull along. No, the rat on its back holds a twig in its teeth and the second rat pulls it by that.'

Egg and rat race

But several correspondents confirmed the tail tow rope bit, and Mr G. Sutton, of Southend-on-Sea, Essex, gave us an eye-witness account with a nice twist:

'In 1909 my grandfather kept a pub called 'The Puss in Boots' at Hazelwood, Derby. He also kept geese. One day my cousin and I heard rustling from the outhouse. Peeping over the half door, we were amazed to see three rats. Two of them were in the goose's nest, rolling out an egg on to the stomach of the third, which wrapped its legs round the egg. One of the others then caught hold of its tail and dragged it towards their hole. However, when they got there; the egg was too big, so we stepped in and rescued it.'

Mr G. Williams, of Haverfordwest, Dyfed, recalled watching rats in a combined operation stealing eggs from a crate in a shop window on an otherwise dull Sunday in Pembroke Dock:

'Seeing a crowd of people looking at this grocer shop window and laughing, I joined them. Two rats were helping themselves to eggs from a crate on a shelf. One rat lay on its back on the floor while the other pushed an egg out of the crate, to be caught deftly between the four paws of the first. The second rat then climbed down and dragged its companion, plus egg, by its tail across the floor to a hole, down which they manoeuvred their prize.'

Mr J. Haworth, of Accrington, Lancs – the same chap who reminded us about Clark Gable hypnotising hens! – drew our attention to another rat ruse:

'One rat lies on its back, gripping the egg between its paws. A second rat gets on top of the first and they lock together in a ball, with the egg against their stomachs. They then roll along, protecting the egg, until they reach their hole.'

False accusation

Another variation, from Mrs Peggy Snelling, of Richmond, Surrey:

'I have never actually seen rats towing each other, but when I lived in a caravan in an orchard in Devon, I had many a laugh watching them "dribble" duck eggs with their noses. When three or four joined in, it was hilarious, especially when the egg landed in a pond. The rats were wonderful swimmers and divers, but they never landed the egg and had to retire disgruntled.

'The farmer accused us of taking the eggs, until I got him to sit in the caravan and watch. Then I took him to the rat run which went up the bank and through a hole in the hedge, at which point the rats let the eggs roll down the other side, to smash on the stones at the bottom. There were umpteen broken shells and unbroken eggs to prove our innocence to the farmer.'

Early fire warning

If all those stories aren't enough to convince you of the rat's high IQ, what do you make of this one? It's down to Mr A. Ward, of Chalfont St Peter, Bucks:

'During the war, when staying on my uncle's farm in Hampshire, I was birds-nesting in a lane when I heard a rustling and squeaking from the other side of the hedge. Then a line of rats appeared, about ten yards long by three deep, led by an old grey rat which had a bunch of straw lengthways in its mouth. I ran to tell my uncle but by the time I found him they had vanished. He said he'd heard of such things, but had never seen it.

'Well, about three nights later two corn stacks on a farm about three miles away were burned down.

'Years later I related the incident to a man who said he'd seen exactly the same thing in North Bucks and three nights later a big barn was burned down.

'Like Ole Man River, those rats must know something!'

We suggested that perhaps they smelled another rat smoking in bed!

Poacher's pooch

Earlier we said that the fox was the supreme poacher of the animal kingdom. But the human poacher's best friend is the lurcher. In his classic work *The Amateur Poacher* Richard Jefferies wrote of the canny canine:

'He is as cunning and wily in approaching his game as if he had a cross of feline nature in his character. Other dogs trust to speed; but the lurcher steals on his prey without a sound. He enters into the purpose of his master, and if any one appears in sight remains quietly in the hedge with the rabbit or leveret in his mouth till a sign bids him approach . . . But the dogs called lurchers nowadays are mostly of degenerate and impure breed; still, even these are capable of a good deal.'

Now we don't know what the parentage of lurchers was in Jefferies's day, but today the most popular crossing appears to be a greyhound father and a collie mother, though some fanciers have different preferences.

Lurcher lessons

We once printed a letter from a reader who was disappointed that her recently acquired fourteen-months-old lurcher did not seem fast enough to catch rabbits. The resulting mailbag proved to be an interesting essay on the training of these born hunters. For example, a Shropshire Lad wrote from Sheldon, Birmingham:

'If the dog has not caught a rabbit by the age of fourteen months, he probably never will. The trouble may be mental – he may at some time in a chase have run into an obstacle, such as a barbed wire fence, which makes him wary.

'Or it could be physical. His legs might be too long, preventing him getting low enough to pick up the rabbit, so that he overruns it. In which case, he would be better after hares, which are higher off the ground.

'But for anyone starting from scratch with a lurcher pup, here are a few tips. Keep it well away from cats, rats and such-like which it will maul – there's nothing worse than trying to skin a chewed-up rabbit.

'It should be taught to retrieve to hand – you don't want to be shouting and dashing all over the place to get the rabbit off him.

'The dog should not be allowed to chase a rabbit until it is seven to eight months old, when it should be fast enough to catch its quarry quickly.

'If not, it will be sure to give tongue, letting everyone in the parish know what you are about and bringing gamekeepers and other nasty people at the double.

'So if your dog doesn't hunt mutely, be prepared to run as fast as he, for you can still end up in court for catching rabbits by this means.

'Incidentally, a cross between a whippet and a Manchester terrier makes a real good lurcher.'

Cross preferences

But D. J. Wingate, writing from Co. Durham, offered somewhat different advice:

'Start by giving the dog a pint of milk and a raw egg beaten together every day. Lots of fresh vegetables with his meat (or beast's tripe) is also beneficial. Forget about rabbits and go after hares, making sure he has at least one chase a day. This will really build his stamina, lungs and muscles, as hares, unlike rabbits, go on very long runs.

'After a dog day's chasing, lock him in the kennel and do not allow anybody to play with him until he has rested. Remember he is not a pet. Keep him outside and don't let him lie about indoors near radiators or fires because when it is cold he will not leave your side and start to whimper, so giving the hares warning.

'My ideal lurcher is one out of a greyhound crossed with a collie crossed with a saluki – they have speed, brains and stamina.'

While P. H., of Grendon, Northants, provided this know-how:

'As a lurcher is basically a greyhound crossed with a hunting dog, it needs plenty of room to pick up speed. So instead of walking round the perimeter of a field, walk across it to give the dog plenty of room to work. Keeping the dog on a slip lead, walk until the prey has been "set", whereupon you both give chase, not letting the dog go until it has definitely seen what it is after.

'Lastly, a hare or rabbit skin rubbed in the dog's face helps to give it that final piece of aggression it needs.'

Readers' rebuke

Following that correspondence, one or two readers took us to task for encouraging what they considered to be a cruel sport. But most lurchers appear to be owned not only for sport, but as pretty efficient providers for the family pot and their use seems to us to be no more cruel than several more 'acceptable' methods of food production.

Piscatorial prestidigitation

One aspect of the poacher's art about which the uninitiated are invariably sceptical is the taking of trout by the 'tickling' method. We Old Pair have met many a rustic who has claimed to have taken trout by sleight of hand. Likewise we have read accounts of trout tickling in books whose authors we've no reason to doubt. But we have never actually seen it done.

So when a reader asked us to confirm that it is possible to catch wild trout in an open stream by this method, we could only say that we had an open mind on the subject. Which was as good as an open invitation to trout ticklers to reveal all!

Charles Large, a countryman by adoption, wrote from Draycott, Somerset:

'I was evacuated to Somerset from the east end of London during the war. Not long after I arrived I was drafted into a team of nine boys who met on the village bridge after school. The three biggest boys got into the water and, with three smaller boys on either bank, we moved upstream. As the waders disturbed the water, trout scuttled upstream. Our job on the bank was to pinpoint hiding places, whereupon the bigger boys slipped an arm into the hiding place, slowly waving their fingers.

'Upon touching a fish, the first finger and thumb gently sought the open gills while the other fingers tickled the belly. If there was no sudden movement the fish would stay put as long as you tickled.

'Thumb and finger were worked slowly into the gills until they could be closed and the trout hoisted smartly out.

'Our trip covered two miles of the brook to the next hamlet, where we would repair to the road for the journey home. Our catch was sold at fourpence for big 'uns, sixpence for whoppers!

'Funny, but I don't see kids in that brook nowadays. Come to that, I don't see trout there either.'

Gently does it

Obviously pollution had put paid to the few Charles and his accomplices didn't catch. However, his letter recalled a blissful childhood spent in the Shetland Isles for James Ridland, of Ilkeston, Derbyshire:

'Here's how I tickled trout fifty years ago. First find a trout which is stationary, heading upstream and near the left bank – if you are righthanded.

'Approach with great caution, lie on the bank, reach down and break the surface of the water very gently with your right hand. If the fish remains still after this, you have overcome the greatest difficulty. The point of touch is behind the right pectoral fin.

'Make sure your fingers rub on contact. I have seen a fish roll over in my hand in what appeared to be ecstasy. With thumb and forefinger you grab the fish by the gills and – hey presto! – it's yours.'

Some trout-ticklers offered a word of warning – mind you don't tickle a water rat or crayfish, both of which can give a nasty nip. And Mrs J. Rees, of Newcastle Emlyn, Dyfed, reported tickling a 3lb sea trout, which, as we Old Pair know, would be a handful to catch by any method.

POW poacher

But the fishy story which tickled us Old Pair most came from Mr J. Crossley, of South Ockenden, Essex:

'During the Second World War I was in a POW camp at a beautiful place called Lindewiese in the Sudetenland. The German Feldwebel in charge was quite a good guy. On Sunday afternoons he allowed us to go for walks.

'Noticing fish darting about in a stream, Sgt Stan Leworthy, 2nd Battalion Dorsetshire Regiment, said: "How would you like some fish for tea?" He then stripped off, got into the water and told me to walk slowly along the bank and note where the fish darted as he walked against the current. When I pointed out where a fish had gone, he laid down in the icy water, arms outstretched. In a short while he came up with a trout in each hand. This he did several times.

'The trout were delicious but the smell roused the Germans who wanted to see our nets. They wouldn't believe the Sarge had caught them with his hands and the Feldwebel said he would come to watch next Sunday. In fact, the whole village turned out to see the Englander catch fish with his bare hands, and Sgt Leworthy obliged with twelve.

'We exchanged four fish for a bag of dog-ends and cigar butts. After that we were well in with the Feldwebel, who sent for us whenever he fancied fish.'

Angler's anguish

That letter proved to be a delightful surprise for Mrs D. Buckingham, of South Molton, Devon, for Sgt Stan Leworthy was her father. Sadly, he had died some four years before Mr Crossley wrote to us but it brought back happy memories for his daughter:

'He often told the story of the POW camp fishing expeditions and was once challenged to prove that it could be done. So one Sunday we all went to the river, Dad waded in and we kept a look-out. Eventually we saw a fish dart under tha bank and before long Dad came up triumphant – not with a trout but with a salmon!

'Another time, when on a picnic, Dad felt sorry for a man who had been fishing all afternoon, without a bite. So he knelt on the bank, leaned over, felt around, and produced a large trout. This he presented to the poor angler – who was lost for words!'

As frustrated fishermen ourselves, we reckoned that angler was speechless as much from indignation as gratitude, but we'd have loved to have seen his face.

AUTO SUGGESTIONS

BY RIGHTS, this chapter should have been included in our Little Black Book No. 3. At least, such was the idea of the reader who suggested it. That was in October, 1976, when Mr V. Cornacia of Plymouth wrote:

'As a young lad in the early 1930s I had a two-year spell in a Welsh village hospital. Most of that time was spent in an adult ward where many of the elder patients took on the role of teacher, to help my interrupted education. Among their pearls of wisdom, I remembered most of all the following toast:

Here's to a friend, pray keep him so
But do not let that friend your secrets know.
For if that friend becomes your foe,
Then all the world your secrets know.

'Perhaps other readers may know of similar toasts, which would make a fine contribution to your Little Black Book Number Three.'

But by then we had already written much of our third volume and we simply did not have time to include the scores of homespun epigrams – the stuff of which autograph albums are made – which poured in.

Indeed, we had room to publish only a comparatively small proportion in the Live Letters page but we asked our lass Lottie to file them all for us and – wonder of wonders! – she has been able to unearth them. So now we offer a fuller selection.

Prim and improper

They fall into various categories, from the Victorian and virtuous to the downright saucy, but we have put them in no particular order – we simply present them as a random read for your delectation and delight. And we hope that some of them you may find useful when next you are confronted with the pristine page of a friend's or relative's autograph album and asked to inscribe something witty or wise.

The young lass responsible for this one must have been a thoroughly modern miss of her times. It was sent in by C. Carless, of Bromborough, Wirral, who told us:

'Fifty years ago, on my sixteenth birthday, I was given an autograph album and the first person I asked to write in it was an 18-year-old girl friend. Here is what she wrote:

As a rule, a man's a fool,
When it's hot he wants it cool.
When it's cool he wants it hot –
Always wanting what it's not.'

Tit for Tat

The battle of the sexes is reflected in many of the contributions. This next one could have been written by way of reply to the last:

Here's to good old whisky
So sparkling and so clear.
Not half so sweet as woman's lips,
But a d- - - - - sight more sincere.

We reckon some poor bloke wrote that on the rebound from a scotched romance!

Curiously, it was sent to us by a woman, as were these misogynistic efforts:

A thousand years ago today,
When a wilderness was here,
A man with powder in his gun
Went forth to hunt a deer.
But times have altered somewhat,
And on a different plan,
A dear with powder on her nose
Goes forth to hunt a man.

Little dabs of powder,
Little bits of paint
Make a woman's features
What they really ain't.

And how about this for cynicism?

Here's to the girl in high heel shoes
Who smokes your fags and drinks your booze,
And then goes home to her mother to snooze.

But perhaps we should let the ladies have the last word in this respect:

Women have many faults
Men have only two –
Everything they say,
And everything they do!

Way to a man's heart

Now let's strike a less acrimonious note with a couple of domestic commentaries:

Here's to the girl who can dance like a dream,
To the saint, and the sweet little sinner;
But here's to the best little girl of them all –
The girl who can cook a good dinner!

Which inspired Mrs Dodie Clarke, of North London, to compose her own 'way to a girl's heart':

Here's to the guy who's never too shy
To say we look great– when we do.
But here's to the gem, who's a man among men
Who can cope with the chores – when we've flu!

That amused our ever-lovings, though we did think their laugh a trifle hollow.

Risqué rhymes

Many of the entries in older albums, though perhaps tame by modern standards, must have caused a few blushes and sniggers at the time they were written.

For example, Mrs T. Collyer, of West Hougham, Kent, wrote:

'How about this one, from my grandmother's autograph album, dated 1909?

Here lies the body of Betsy Sims
Who was so very pure within
She cracked the outer shell of sin
And hatched herself a cherubim!'

Is the permissive society really all that new? asked Mrs Collyer. Of course not, but we reckoned her grandma's friends may have been more forward-thinking than most young ladies around 1909.

Or were they? Mrs E. T., of Wotton-under-Edge, Glos, wrote:

'In my fifty-eight-year-old album I found a very saucy verse, written by a saucy fella, which would not have meant much in the mini-skirt era:

Here's to the breezes that blow through the treezes
And blow their clothes over young ladies' kneezes.
Here's to the man who can see what he pleases –
Lace, garters, drawers and even chemises.

Several readers submitted this, in similar vein:

The Devil made the wind to blow
The Ladies' skirts so high,
But God was just and made the dust
To blow in the bad man's eye.

As one reader put it, 'It was considered very naughty' – but at least it had the redeeming factor of retribution.

Sitting joke

Joan Davies, of Brighton, recalled that this one, written in her album some fifty years ago, caused much fun:

That fellow George comes round too much,
Said Mary's father, grim.
The next time he comes round this way,
You must sit down on him.
Now Mary's an obedient child,
She used her worldly powers,
The next time George came visiting
She sat on him three hours!

And we can imagine the titters evoked by this one, recalled by Mrs M. Snowdon, of Ormskirk:

He tried it on the sofa
He tried it on the chair
He tried it on the window ledge
But couldn't get it there.
He tried this way and that way
And ways that'd make you laugh
Just to make his girlfriend smile –
While he took her photograph.

Romantic nonsense

Our next three offerings reflect the vicissitudes of love. The first, under the heading 'The Arithmetic Lesson', was written more than sixty years ago in the album of Mrs Day, Sidcup.

He was teaching her arithmetic;
He said it was his mission.
He kissed her once, he kissed her twice,
And said: 'Now that's addition.'
But as he gave her kiss by kiss,
In silent satisfaction,
She hurriedly gave him one back,

And said; 'Now that's subtraction.'
But presently her Pa came by,
And snorting with derision,
Kicked poor John three streets away,
And said; 'That's long division'.

Mrs Day told us that the album is now treasured by her grandchildren – and that's multiplication.

This rather bitter little story of unrequited love appears to have been curiously popular:

Go to Father, she said when I asked her to wed,
For she knew that I knew that her father was dead.
And she knew that I knew what a life he had led.
So she knew that I knew what she meant when she said,
Go to Father!

While not exactly Shakespeare, here's a tragicomedy enacted in eight lines:

With all a lover's courtly air
He placed upon her satin chair,
Where she would sit so fresh and fair,
A Rose.
Now love is dead and life's forlorn
No rose there is without a thorn,
For down she sat and then with scorn,
Arose.

Riddle of love

Verily, as the poet said, the course of true love ne'er did run smooth. However, it's nice to have a happy ending occasionally and here's a lovely one, from Mrs D. Hopkins, of Driffield:

'At the age of sixteen, I treasured my autograph book, but being a shy girl, I was too bashful to ask my boyfriend for his longed-for autograph. At last, during his summer vacation from boarding school, I summoned up the courage and loaned him my autograph book. This is what my eager eyes beheld on its return:

There was a little man,
His name was Henry Ford.
He got a bit of piping
And a little bit of cord.

A little drop of petrol
In an old tin can.
He put it all together,
And the damned thing ran.

'I was most hurt, and hid my autograph book away and decided I no longer wanted him for a boyfriend. I kept out of his way until just prior to his return to boarding school, by which time I was feeling sad.

'I brought my autograph book out, and turning the pages I noticed he had written not one autograph but two. The second one read:

Love as one and down and you do
in you but that read you love you
Am will love is up will I love
I see I thee read see that me?

'Imagine my joy when I worked that out!

'We married during the war, and later had three children. Glad to say, I have a sense of humour. Hence this letter to you.'

Our lass Lottie reckons that, personally, she would have needed more than a sense of humour – the poor girl is still trying to work that second entry out!

Cryptic question

Now for another teaser which no doubt gave some Mama the vapours when she discovered it in her daughter's album more than sixty years ago:

When summer suns are past and gone,
Shall autumn suns succeed.
I long to ease my weary mind,
Sleep is the friend I need.
With these few precepts in my mind,
You will in this a question find,
My question's plain, so find it out,
Love is a torment without a doubt.

Fortunately the cheeky chappie who sent us that one gave us a clue – 'First things first' – but he forbore to tell us if he got a satisfactory answer to his question!

Possibly this one revived memories of a schoolgirl crush for Leslie, in whose album it was inscribed in 1923 by her schoolmaster:

A fee simple,
A simple fee
And all the fees entail,
Are nothing when compared to thee,
Thou best of fees – female!

Potty passion

And perchance an old flame came to mind for the gent who wrote to us:

'Harking back to my younger days at the beginning of the century, I well remember writing the following in a young lady's album:

I wish I were the china cup
From which you drink your tea,
Then every sip you took,
I know, would be a kiss from me.'

The soppy suitor who dreamed this one up must have got it really bad to have committed it to paper:

I wish I were a daisy,
All damp and wet with dew,
Then if a cow should stand on me,
I'd gladly die for you.

He was wet all right! And how about this piece of inanity –

My love is like a cabbage,
And to prove to you it's true,
The leaves I give to others
But the heart I give to you.

To round off this amorous anthology, a word – or words – of caution;

Don't go kissing at the garden gate.
Love may be blind – but the neighbours ain't!

Which reminds us of that other popular one:

Never make love in a cornfield – even wheat has ears!

Moral boosters

Having read thus far – at least, we hope you have – you may have gained the impression that our collection of autograph album entries deals only with the lighter side of life. Prepare to be disabused! By far the greater number we received were high-toned epigrams, such as might have been penned by maiden aunts or proud fathers as guide lines to instruct lads and lasses in the good conduct of life.

Again they might be considered naive and 'corny' by modern youth, but nonetheless they were inscribed with sincerity and, as many of their recipients confirmed to us, proved their worth over the years.

For example, we had scores of copies of this one:

Your future lies before you,
Like a sheet of driven snow.
Be careful how you tread it,
For every mark will show.

The entry in Swanscombe reader Mrs Joyce Fuller's album was signed 'Mother, Dec 25, 1932'. Joyce commented, 'Glad to say I have a clean sheet.' A popular variation of the same idea:

May your life be like a snowflake –
Leave a mark but not a stain.

Old school tie

Sometimes mention of a certain piece in our column causes particular delight for another reader for whom it has its own personal significance. Such was the case when we printed the following:

Good, Better, Best,
Never let it rest –
Until your Good is Better,
And your Better, Best.

Seventy-year-old Mrs Lillian Haynes, of Worcester, wrote:

'You can imagine my feelings when I saw my old school motto in Live Letters. It was slightly different – "never let us rest, till our Good is Better". And our maxim was – "If each outside his own door swept, the city would be clean". The school was St John's Girls School, Bromyard Road, Worcester. A wonderful school, and I went right through it from the age of five to fourteen. I get much pleasure from Live Letters, but never such a thrill as now.'

Happy compromise

The less competitive spirits among you will no doubt prefer the more compromising course suggested in this verse, found by Mrs Evelyn Slingsby, of Windsor, in an album dated 1903:

Do what you can, being what you are,
Shine like a glowworm, if you cannot like a star.
Work as a pulley if you cannot as a crane,
Be a wheel greaser, if you cannot drive the train.

A note in Mrs Slingsby's album said it was 'taken from an American paper'.

Good and bad

There were many variations on the theme of do-as-you-would-be-done-by, the most popular being this one which Mrs D. Wright, of North Finchley, told us her father always wrote when presented with an album:

There is so much bad in the best of us,
There is so much good in the worst of us
That it ill-behoves any of us
To find fault with the rest of us.

And on the same lines:

Speak no ill, but lenient be
To others' failings as your own,
If you're the first a fault to see,
Be you the last to make it known.

Or:

Do not look for faults as you go through life,
And even when you find them,
It is wise and kind to be sometimes blind,
And look for the virtues behind them.

Mind you, equally as popular as the first of those three was this tongue-twisting piece of defiant self-respect:

Here's to you as good as you are,
And here's to me as bad as I am
But as good as you are and as bad as I am,
I'm as good as you are – as bad as I am!

Droll doggerel

An ode to owlish wisdom is the favourite inscription of Jon Haerem, of London W9:

A wise old owl lived in an oak,
The more he saw, the less he spoke.
The less he spoke, the more he heard,
Why can't we be like that wise old bird?

Jon suggested that a copy should be sent to every

politician and disc jockey in the land!

We must admit that we prefer our homespun philosophy when it is served with a dash of wry humour. Like this, from Mrs Lilian Doble, of Loughton:

There are many ways of doing things,
As everybody supposes.
Some folks turn up their sleeves at work,
And some turn up their noses.

From Doreen Pink, of Havant:

When very young as I recall,
I truly thought I knew it all.
But now it seems, as old I grow,
The more I see, the less I know!

And from Hylda Ball, of Crewe:

What's got without effort
Is worth what it cost.
Things easily gained
Are things easily lost.
When a road is worn flat
You can bet your best hat
That it leads to a place
Where too many are at!

Wary words

A couple of cautionary notes with a nice touch of irony, first from Mrs Ivy Phillips, of Bexleyheath:

A fellow feeling is wondrous kind,
Perhaps the poet may change his mind
When in a crowd he may hap find,
A fellow feeling in his coat behind.

And from Mrs M. Mawby, of Rickmansworth:

Since man to man is so unjust,
I hardly know which one to trust.
I've trusted many to my sorrow,
So pay me today and I'll trust you tomorrow.

While another with a 'once-bitten' feeling to it was supplied by Mrs Iris Cowlbeck, of Runwell, Essex:

Men are moulded just the same,
A happy band of brothers.
The only difference is that some
Are mouldier than others.

Bessie's dream

After that somewhat jaundiced view of human nature, an altogether more optimistic note. It was entered in the album of Mrs J. Andrews, of Bedlington, when she was fourteen, by the late Bessie Braddock, Labour MP for the Exchange Division of Liverpool for some twenty-five years.

Good folks all, a word with you,
What a world to bring us to.
But we will make the world anew,
Boys and girls together.
We are children, but some day,
We'll be big and strong and say:
None shall slave and none shall slay,
All shall work together.

On top of the verse was written: 'From a Socialist Sunday School Song.' Mrs Andrews commented:

'As far as I can see, we may be together, but we are still waiting for that better world.'

Possibly, but big-hearted Bessie would have been the first to admit that the world can't be renovated overnight. She would also have approved of this one, from Mrs Florence Swainsbury, of Kilburn:

Don't judge the man by the coat he wears,
Or the money he has to back it.
For there's many a true and noble heart
Lies under a ragged jacket.

Think about it

An enigmatic epigram on the fickleness of Dame Fortune was entered in the album of M. Wellington, of Hornchurch, who admits: 'Being a trifle dim, I took some time to put its meaning into perspective. The line was: "As you travel up the road to Prosperity, may you never meet an old friend coming down."'

Mark Twain refers to that one as 'an old time toast which is golden for its beauty.'

Keep smiling

No need to pause for thought over these next exhortations. From Mrs V. Goode, of Kitts Green, Birmingham:

Take care that the face which looks out from

your mirror in the morning is a pleasant one.
You may not see it again all day but others will.

A similar one, from Winifred Taylor, of Paignton:

If your face wants to smile, let it.
If it won't, make it –
It costs nothing to smile!

And, still on smiling, from Albert Bennett, of Plymouth:

It is easy enough to be pleasant,
As life goes by on a song,
But the one worthwhile
Is the one who can smile,
When everything goes dead wrong.

Friendly advice

Nor is there anything complicated about these observations on friendship, both submitted by several readers:

True friends are like diamonds –
Precious and rare.
False friends are like autumn leaves –
Found everywhere.

And:

Choose not your friends by outward show
Feathers float, but pearls lie low.

Mementoes mori

Many readers contributed lines from their albums in the mistaken belief that they were original compositions by their fathers or other relatives. A case in point is this pithy epigram on inevitability cum resignation: 'Nothing is more certain than death and taxes.'

At least two readers thought this had been coined by their clever Dads. In fact it is a paraphrase of an observation by Benjamin Franklin, the 18th century American statesman and philosopher: 'In this world nothing can be said to be certain, except death and taxes.'

Charles Dickens used a variation on Franklin's quote in *David Copperfield* where Mr Barkis says: 'It was as true as taxes is. And nothing's truer than them.'

An expansion of the idea, from the album of Mrs Edna Simpson, of Huddersfield:

Life is a theatre, so they say,

With low and lofty places.
And in the world, as in the play,
Are various forms and faces.
But when Life's comedy is over
And Death rings down the curtain,
All pass out at the common door,
And that alone is certain.

Somehow the version provided by Mr J. Hoare, of Bootle, seems all the more sombre for its brevity:

As the leaf doth fall,
So shall we all
After youth, and bloom, have gone.

Ironic entry

But in none of those we received is the approach of the Grim Reaper referred to more poignantly than in the following example from Mrs D. Wills, of Ryde, Isle of Wight. She told us:

'When I was twelve, a school pal wrote in my autograph book this verse:

Here's to the world as round as a wheel,
The sting of death we all must feel.
But if Life was a thing that money could buy,
The rich would live and the poor would die.

'Unfortunately I lost sight of my pal after leaving school, but heard years later that she had died from TB in her early twenties.'

Ours not to reason . . .

For some, the questions raised by such tragedies are best left unasked. As this verse, from Mrs A. Smith, of Thornton Heath, puts it:

Not until the looms are silent
And the shuttles cease to fly,
Will God unroll the pattern
And explain the reason why
The dark threads are as needful
In the weaver's skilful hands
As the gold threads and the silver
In the pattern that he plans.

Here's a little light relief, though still in deadly earnest, which cropped up more than once:

A man is not old when his hair turns grey.
A man is not old when his teeth decay.
But it is time he went to his last long sleep,
When his mind makes appointments his body can't keep!

If that means what we think it means, we Old Pair have stayed up long past our bedtime!

Old favourites

Before we get too flippant, here are a few more 'serious' ones which, if only by dint of their popularity, must be included.

You can't beat the good old 'uns, as Mr T. Hallett, of Odcombe, Somerset, put it, his 'little gem' being:

It's not the ones who say the most
Who have the most to say,
And not the ones who have the most
Who give the most away.

Another timeless gem, originally penned by Horace Mann, the 19th century American philanthropist:

Lost, yesterday, somewhere between sunrise and sunset,
Two golden hours, each set with sixty diamond minutes.
No reward is offered, for they are gone forever.

Similarly:

If you in the morning
Throw minutes away,
You can't pick them up
In the course of the day.

Trouble shooter

One we have also seen in countless Christmas cracker mottoes:

Never trouble trouble
'Til trouble troubles you
Or you'll only double trouble
And trouble others too.

In fact, the origin of that one was 'Trouble', a poem by David Keppel, another American religious writer of the mid-19th century:

Better never trouble Trouble
Until Trouble troubles you,
For you only make your trouble
Double-trouble when you do,
And the trouble – like a bubble –
That you're troubling about,
May be nothing but a cipher,
With its rim rubbed out.

And one for every Mum to remember when she is stumped for something appropriate:

As you journey on life's way,
If you are tempted to go astray,
It won't take a minute,
It won't take a day,
To stop and think
What Mother would say.

Not so serious, this one from Miss E. Edwards, of Cheltenham, but a shrewd comment on a feeling most of us have known at some time or another:

How very nice it is to see
Our dear relations come to tea.
But nicer still it is to know,
That when they've had their tea they'll go!

That must have been written on a Sunday evening after a visit from an unfavourite aunt.

Witty but inane

Now we turn from the sublime (?) to the ridiculous with a selection of the dottier jottings and literary lunacies which have their place in every autograph album and, we hope, nowhere else!

Starting with the inevitable:

2 Ys U R
2 Ys U B
I C U R
2 Ys 4 ME

Clever stuff indeed. And the classic:

The lightning flashed,
The thunder roared,
And all the world was shaken,
A little pig cocked up his tail

And ran to save his bacon.

Running that close for poetic inspiration must be:

I stood on the bridge at midnight
When a thought came into my head
What a fool I was to be standing there
When I might have been in bed.

A couple of inanities contributed by Mrs C. Baldwin, of London E15:

The rabbit has a shiny nose,
On that you can depend,
Because his little powder puff
Is at the other end.

I eat peas with honey,
I've done it all my life.
It may taste rather funny
But it keeps them on the knife.

Fom bad to verse

And two from Mrs Anne Benson, of Northampton:

Hands up, hands up, the robber cried,
Hand over all your riches,
I can't, I can't, the victim cried
I'm holding up my breeches!

Adam and Eve in the garden stood,
Viewing the beautiful nature.
The devil looked out from a gooseberry bush
And hit Eve in the eye with a tater.

More potty poetry about Adam and Eve:

Good morning, Madam, to Eve said Adam,
Good morning, Sir, to him said her.

Adam and Eve in the garden of Eden
In summer time they were jolly.
But what did they do in the winter time,
When there were no leaves but holly?

Adam was the first man
Samson was the strongest

Of all the birds that fly in the air,
The monkey's tail is the longest.

Basic humour

To round off these ridiculous rhymes, two rib-ticklers. First:

You may speak of the joys of summer
Of winter you may sing,
But to sit down quick on a red hot brick,
Is the sign of an early spring.

We'd just recovered from that one, when Mrs Rosina Lower, of London SW18, told us:

'When I was a little girl, someone wrote in my autograph book:

Sweet little Emily Rose,
Was tired and sought to repose,
But her sister named Clare
Put a tack on her chair –
Sweet little Emily rose!

'It wasn't until some years later that I realised why Emily rose!'

We're surprised that, with a name like Rosina, she didn't get the point sooner!

Blank verse

As we said at the beginning of this chapter, we hope this miscellany will provide some ideas the next time you are asked to write something appropriate or clever in an album. But if you've found nothing suitable in the foregoing, and are still stumped, don't worry. Make a virtue of the fact, as the perpetrators of these pungent pieces did.

From P. McGinnes, of Wavertree, Liverpool:

I want to write something original
I don't know how to begin.
For there's only one thing original in me
And that's original sin.

From E. Horwood, of Sidley, Bexhill-on-Sea, Sussex:

Head thick, brain dumb,
Inspiration won't come.
Can't write, bad pen,
Yours truly, Amen.

From Suzanne Haley, of Sutton Coldfield:

I sat and thought and tried to think,
I dipped my pen into the ink,
I sat and thought but nothing came
So I thought I'd write my name.

One which, as Mrs W. Driver, of Burnley, Lancs, points out, always sets the reader counting:

The owner of this book
Asks for a word or two from me
But as I'm in a generous mood
I've written twenty-three.

Or should it be twenty-four?

More tricky stuff, which turned up from several sources:

You ask for something original,
For something out of my head.
I can't think of anything inside,
So I give from the outside instead.

And attached is a lock of the writer's hair.

G. Dumbrell, of Steyning, Sussex, was one of many who sent in:

When in this book you look
And on the page you frown,
Think of the one who spoiled your book
By writing upside down.

Needless to say, the writer had first turned the album upside down.

Parting shots

Equally popular among the clever-clever variety is the last page entry:

By hook or by crook
I'll be last in your book.

In the album owned by Amelia Pass, of Newcastle, Staffs, that had been capped by someone writing on the very edge of the last page:

Not so fast my friend
I am the end.

But for real one-upmanship, how about this? We had almost completed this chapter when the following arrived from Mrs Sheila Woolf, of London E4:

'When my son left junior school last year, his headmaster wrote in his autograph book: "Salamu Sana Na Kwaheri." So far we have been unable to find out what it means. Can you help?'

We could, though our Swahili was a trifle rusty, A fair translation would be 'Greetings and farewell'. Swahili is a language spoken in East Africa – and, apparently, in East London!

Dire warning

Of the front-page cautions against stealing the album, we liked this one most:

Steal not this book, mine honest friend,
Lest the gallows be thine end,
And when you're dead the Lord will say
Where is that book you took away?
Then if you say you do not know,
He will cast you down below.

It certainly had the desired effect on G. Godfrey, of Bridgend, Mid-Glam, who told us:

'I can't remember who wrote it, but ever since I've had a dread of stealing, books especially.'

Treasured memories

But no matter what the nature of the entries – serious or silly, instructive or inane – the real purpose and pleasure of an autograph album is in the mementoes it provides of friends and family, loved ones and lost ones.

Mrs Joan Atherson, of Warndon, Worcester, had these apposite lines:

Your album is your garden plot
Where all your friends may sow
And I, too, in this pleasant spot
Would sow the seed forget-me-not

I write not here for fancy,
I write not here for fame,
I write to be remembered,
And thus inscribe my name

This letter, from Mr J. Haworth, of Accrington, Lancs, makes the point touchingly:

'This verse, written in my album years ago, makes me feel sad when I read it now:

Perchance in some far distant year,
When on this page thine eyes may fall,
This message lightly written here,
May memories of the past recall.

'It was signed simply "Mother". She died nine years ago.'

We are grateful to Mrs M. Morse, of Barry, S. Glamorgan, not only for the Welsh verse which, as she says, 'sums up all autograph sentiment put together', but for the English translation:

How pleasant to look in the album in the years to come. You will see the handwriting of many a friend who is now too far to shake your hand.

Mrs Morse added her own comment: 'How very true – after nearly sixty years in this vale of tears, I can think of nearly a score of friends, relatives and acquaintances who, alas, are either no longer with us, or else too far away to greet personally.'

SCOTS WHA HAE

'I HAVE been trying all my life to like Scotchmen,' wrote Charles Lamb, 'and am obliged to desist from the experiment in despair.' He was only one of several English authors who found that the Scots, like poteen, were a bit much to stomach!

Hazlitt was equaly critical, commenting, 'The Scotch, as a nation, are particularly disagreeable. They hate every appearance of comfort themselves and refuse it to others. Their climate, their religion and their habits are equally averse to pleasure. Their manners are either distinguished by a fawning sycophancy (to gain their own ends, and to conceal their natural defects) that makes one sick; or by a morose, unbending callousness, that makes one shudder.'

Dr Johnson, who, in Boswell, recognised that the Scots, like the curate's egg, were not all entirely bad, was better humoured in the way he poked fun at those north of the border. 'The noblest prospect which a Scotchman ever sees,' said he, 'is the high road that leads him to England.' Another time, he remarked: 'Seeing Scotland, Madam, is only seeing a worse England.' And again: 'Their learning is like bread in a besieged town; every man gets a little, but no man gets a full meal.'

The Great Lexicographer also defined oats as a commodity used in Scotland to feed men, but in England to feed horses – to which Boswell riposted: 'But did you ever see such men or such horses?'

That celebrated wit, Sydney Smith, jested: 'It requires a surgical operation to get a joke well into a Scotch understanding.' In this, he echoed the sentiment of a derisory Scots poem, *The Pawky Duke*, which said that to get a joke into that particular aristocrat's cranium, it would have to be trepanned!

However, the Scots themselves have proved no mean hands at nationalist banter. The nineteenth century writer, Christopher North, conversing with the Ettrick Shepherd, James Hogg, commented: 'Minds like ours, my dear James, must always be above national prejudices, and in all companies it gives me true pleasure to declare, that, as a people, the English are very little indeed inferior to the Scotch.' And of the Danish invasion of England, it was remarked: 'The acute Angles went north, and the obtuse Angles stayed south!'

So much for the badinage. Nowadays, ancestral animosities are largely forgotten (except at Hampden Park or Wembley!) and increasing numbers of the English, as well as of other races, are reversing Johnson's trend and taking the high road north to make the Grand Tour of Scotland. Their inquiries, and comments, form the basis for this chapter.

Porridge drawers

We got our sporrans in a right twist over this particular subject, for, not having come across this phenomenon on our many sojourns up north, we wrongly concluded that it was a leg-pull. In fact, the question of porridge drawers last year created a greater stir in our column than any oatmeal swirling in a tureen.

It all started with a letter from Mrs Susan Barton, of Grays, Essex, who wrote: 'A chap at work swears that in the remote parts of Scotland it is an old custom to have a porridge drawer. According to him, porridge is made up as thick as a cake and poured into a special drawer to be offered to guests!' She added that he was prepared to stake his next week's wages on the truth of the story. Regrettably, we dismissed this culinary delight as pure fiction, comparing it to spaghetti trees and treacle mines.

That did it! Like sacks of oatmeal from a mill, the mail-bags poured in, correcting us. One reader even suggested we should do porridge! Ah well, when you boob, you can only make the reply that Dr Johnson gave to a lady who spotted a mistake in his famous dictionary, 'Ignorance, madam, pure ignorance!'

Weekly ritual

Mrs D. Medhurst, of Windsor, Berks, who lived on a farm in Fife during the last war, had a shepherd as neighbour. Each week, he had a large drawer removed from the kitchen table and scrubbed white. While it dried, the porridge was cooked in a large pan. After it cooled, it was poured into the drawer and allowed to solidify. When the shepherd set off for the hills, often on a two or three day outing, he would take a knife, spoon, billycan and a large slice of porridge. He would get water from a burn and make a sustaining breakfast.

Angus MacPhee, of Birmingham, confirmed the custom,

writing that, in his younger days, he would join company in a bothy (farmworkers' hut) where ballads were sung to the accompaniment of a fiddle, mouth-organ or button-key accordion. At half-time, slices of porridge were handed round, ensuring more hilarity and a good night's sleep, since they had been laced wi' a drappie o' the auld crater!

Mr H. Smith, of Dartford, Kent, gave us further information, describing how, well over sixty years ago, he was reared in a Scots colony at the Bottom Farm, Berkhamsted, Herts. There were Campbells there, Craigs, Hoys and McCoys, all of whom could run up and down granary steps carrying 2½cwt sacks of wheat, all day, without batting an eyelid. Their staple diet was oatmeal, made from chaff blowings or husks, steeped in huge cauldrons of water to ferment. In a few days, there was a mass of stinking foam on top but, when this had settled, the resultant gel was boiled for some hours. When cooled, it was cut into slices and stored in drawers until needed. It was then warmed up in a saucepan and salted.

Mr Smith added: 'That concoction put hairs on the chest, roses in the cheeks, and biceps like rugger balls on the arms. But best of all, it didn't cost muckle!'

Other readers, whose contributions we didn't have room to print, pointed out that marauding Highland clansmen regularly carried porridge on their forays. They kept it in a pouch, forerunner of the sporran. In more recent days, weavers, miners and other early risers resorted to the porridge drawer to save time.

Down the hatch!

One correspondent, whose husband was on army training in the Ben Nevis area during the war, told us of a gillie whose breakfast invariably consisted of porridge and a stiff glass of whisky. The gillie was 82 at the time but had better eyesight and stamina than the Special Air Service men involved in the manoeuvres. Obviously a spirited character!

Top drawer

A joiner added a further piece of technical information. He told us the porridge drawer was the top, left-hand one in a Scotch dresser, being the only one to be sealed with hot glue to prevent leakage. He personally had repaired many.

Incidentally, a typical example of a dresser (or 'girnal' or 'kist', as it was called) can be found in the Burns Bachelor Club, on the Burns Trail at Tarbolton, near Ayr. A Worcester visitor to the Club, founded by Burns and now Scottish National Trust property, had this verse recited to him by the guide:

May ye aye be just as happy as I wish you aye to be,
May a mouse ne'er leave your girnal with a tear drop in its e'e,
May ye aye keep hale and hearty till ye're auld enough to dee.

And on that philosophic reflection about Mice and Scotsmen, we'll close this particular subject, merely recording our gratitude to all who taught us Sassenachs to eat humble pie and know our oats better the next time!

Drop outs

Speaking of porridge, we can't resist referring to the celebrated, if entirely mythical, 'spoon heap' at Berwick-on-Tweed. This is supposed to be the accumulation of porridge spoons thrown out of trains by Scots heading for the golden pavements of London. As J. M. Barrie remarked, 'There are few more impressive sights in the world than a Scotsman on the make!'

Great chieftain

From porridge to haggis – that succulent dish which Burns described as 'Great chieftain o' the puddin'-race'. We've been asked a few times what it consists of. As it happens, a few years back, one of our everlovings received a colourful tea-towel in her Christmas stocking depicting 'Mrs McLeod's Original Haggis'. Here are the basic ingredients: 'One sheep's pluck and bag, quarter pound of suet, two onions, black pepper, salt and a half teaspoonful of mixed herbs'.

The good lady's instructions for cooking are: 'Wash bag in cold water, and bring to boil. Scrape and clean, leave overnight. Mince heart, lights and liver (that's the "pluck"). Add toasted oatmeal, chopped suet, and onions. Season highly with black pepper, salt and herbs. Fill bag and sew up, allowing for swelling. Place in hot water and boil for three hours'. As one Scots grocer told us, 'A repast fit to grace the table of a Princess!'

Water of life

The haggis, of course, is the 'pièce de résistance' at Burns Suppers, which commemorate the birth of the poet on January 25, 1759 – a tradition presumably founded by the first Burns Club, which was formed in 1801, nearly five years after his death. The haggis is borne in by the chef to the accompaniment of bagpipes; the address to it is declaimed; and it is then downed with copious stoups of whisky. We recall that at one Supper we attended, the chef, who had drunk if not wisely at least well before emerging from the kitchen, instead of plunging the knife into the pudding, made an unfortunate stab at amputating his hand – to unkind laughter from one or two quarters!

And that brings us to whisky, a word derived from the Gaelic 'uiscebeatha', itself a translation of the Latin 'aqua vitae', the water of life. The spirit was distilled from at least the fifteenth century by Highland crofters, as a by-product of the cultivation of barley. In the Lowlands, the common tipple was 'Twopenny', an ale selling at twopence a Scotch pint. Burns, who liked both beverages, wrote:

Wi' tippeny, we fear nae evil.
Wi' usquebae, we'll face the devil.

'Twopenny' was made from malt, and in 1725 the Government imposed a sixpenny tax on every bushel, sparking off riots in the towns. As a result, the duty was halved, but there was a steep decline in popular demand for the ale, and this opened up the market for whisky, which, until about 1750, was virtually unknown outside the Highlands.

In 1773, Dr Johnson, on his tour to the Hebrides, called for a glass with the words, 'Come, let us know what it is that makes a Scotchman happy!' It probably came from an illicit still. Certainly, as late as 1820, half of Scotland's whisky came from unlicensed stills of which there were 200 in Glenlivet alone. This was the result of the prohibitive duty slapped on the spirit during the Napoleonic wars. Pretty rough stuff most of it must have been – what an American writer John O'Sullivan (1813-1895) was aptly to describe as 'A torchlight procession marching down your throat'.

In 1820, the Duke of Gordon, the greatest landowner in the central Highlands, appealed to the Government to reduce the duty, and an Act of 1823 cut it to 2s 3d a proof gallon. The Act also introduced to Scotland the system of warehousing spirits before payment of duty, and prescribed regulations controlling the distiller's operations. This killed off most illicit stills and ended the smuggling of imported foreign spirits such as French brandy. It was not until 1915, however, that another Act, the Immature Spirits (Restrictive) Act, prohibited the sale of whisky less than three years old.

Stills

There were two kinds of still, the traditional pot-still which was used for malted barley only, and the Coffey still or 'patent-still' which distilled grain whisky and, eventually, a blend of the lighter Lowland malts and grains. The latter was patented by Aeneas Coffey in 1831. The pot-still was originally filled with water by hand, emptied and filled again, a laborious and, in terms of labour, expensive process. But in 1827-28, the foremost distiller in Scotland, Robert Stein, took out a patent for a still heated by steam, instead of by a furnace, which distilled spirit in one continuous process.

Till the middle of the nineteenth century, all whiskies were the product of one distillery only. Then, in the 1860s, blending came into fashion. In 1877, the owners of six Lowland grain distilleries – Cambus, Cameronbridge, Carsebridge, Glenochil, Kirkliston and Port Dundas – opened up the market by forming a trade association with a nominal capital of two million pounds. Thus was born the Distillers Company Limited, with registered offices in Edinburgh. Today there are 45 malt distilleries in Scotland, half on Speyside, and five large grain distilleries. The Company (which kindly provided some of this information) is now the biggest operator in the field.

The London scene

Whisky did not catch on in the London market until the 1880s. Before that, Sir Winston Churchill has recorded, the upper and middle classes seldom touched the stuff. Writing about his father, he said he never drank whisky 'except on a moor or in some very dull and chilly place. He lived in the age of brandy and soda'. However, when phylloxera, an insect pest, ravaged the French vineyards from the 1860s into the next century, brandy was supplanted by blended whisky as the 'in' drink in society.

The first distiller to break into the London market, in 1880, was Alexander Walker of Kilmarnock. He was soon followed by Buchanan, Dewar, Haig and others. By the end of the nineteenth century, a thriving export market had been built up by means of a string of agents throughout the world. Other countries have tried to imitate Scotch. Whisky, for example, was distilled in Wales from the fifteenth century until early this century. The ruins of the last distillery can be seen at Frongoch, near Bala. The Japanese have also tried their hand at producing it, but no country has been really successful. Maybe it's the water from rivers such as the Spey that distinguishes the genuine McCoy!

Maturity is all

Now for some questions about whisky which readers have fired at us. For a start, how is the spirit matured? Ideally in sherry casks. From this, as it matures over a period of years, it absorbs both flavour and natural colour (otherwise colour is added with caramel). Most connoisseurs reckon seven to twelve years in the cask are ideal. Whisky left too long tends to develop a 'woody' taste. Obviously, there aren't enough sherry casks to go round, so most Scotch is now matured in steel containers.

How do blenders determine the right mix? Not by tasting, but by 'nosing' the bouquet.

What is meant by proof spirit? This is a mixture of 57.1% spirit and 42.9% water. Whisky is normally sold in the UK market at 30 degrees under proof. That is to say it contains 40% pure spirit and 60% water. Proof is tested by the Sikes hydrometer, patented by Bartholomew Sikes, Secretary to the Board of Excise. It was universally adopted in 1818.

The origin of the word 'proof' is this. In olden days, whisky and gunpowder were mixed and ignited. If the gunpowder flashed, there was enough whisky in the mixture to permit ignition. If it didn't, the whisky was too weak. Whisky which ignited was said to have been 'proved'.

Price and measure

We are often asked to give some idea of the comparative prices of whisky over the years. Briefly, in 1914, the retail price per bottle varied from 2s 11d to 3s 6d, according to proof. That was for bulk whiskies. Proprietary brands cost between 4s and 4s 6d. The excise duty remained at 14s 9d per proof gallon until 1918, when the Chancellor raised it to 30s. Shortly afterwards, the retail price of a bottle of Scotch was fixed at 9s. In 1919, this went up to 10s 6d when duty was raised to 50s a gallon, and in 1920 to 7s 6d – a figure at which it remained until 1939. The price of a bottle was then 12s 6d. Since then the excise duty has gone up by leaps and bounds, causing the whisky distillers to protest that they are carrying an unfair share of taxation. In 1976, for example, the duty charged per degree of alcoholic strength was 8.59p for beer, 16.25p for imported table wine, 12.62p for imported sherry, but 27.09p for Scotch.

As for measures, strictly speaking a nip can be anything, though generally it is a sixth of a gill in England and Wales, a fifth in Scotland. Bottles are of standard measurements. An imperial quart contains 40 fluid ounces; a standard bottle 26 and two-thirds; a half-bottle 13 and a third; a quarter-bottle 6 and two-thirds; and a miniature bottle two fluid ounces.

A final point on Scotch: the Refreshment Houses Act of 1860 allowed shopkeepers to take out licences for the sale of alcoholic drinks, and by 1900 chains of multiple off-licence shops had been established.

Worse for wear

As this particular section began with Burns Suppers, we'll return to the question of whether the poet was as savage a drinker as some of his critics have made out. Did he, in fact, lurch, besotted, to a drunkard's grave years before his time? The answer is that, by contemporary standards, he wasn't a great imbiber. For one thing, he couldn't hold a vast amount and suffered from diabolical hangovers. As he confessed, 'Hard drinking is the devil with me . . .'

Elsewhere he wrote: 'My head aches miserably. One comfort; I suffer so much just now, in this world, and for last night's debauch, that I shall escape scot-free for it in the world to come – Amen!' And again: 'Regret! Remorse! Shame! ye three hell-hounds that ever dog my steps and bay at my heels, spare me! spare me!' On the other hand he was, in Johnson's phrase, 'a clubbable man', a gregarious drinker who enjoyed a night out in good company and who found that whisky often inspired his pen. As he put it:

O Whisky! soul o' plays and pranks
Accept a Bardie's gratefu' thanks!
When wanting thee, what tuneless cranks
Are my poor verses!
Thou comes – they rattle i' their ranks
At ither's arses.

And on another occasion he penned these jolly lines:

We are na fou, we're nae that fou,
But just a drappie in our e'e!
The cock may craw, the day may daw,
But ay we'll taste the barley-bree!

One of Burns's contemporaries, the Ettrick Shepherd, James Hogg, wrote of him: 'Burns has been accused of inveterate dissipation and drunkenness. Nonsense! Burns was no more of a drunkard than I am; nay, I would take a bet that on an average I drink double of what he did, and yet I am acknowledged both in Scotland and in England, as a most temperate and cautious man; and so I am.' Mind you, the testimony of Hogg might carry a bit more weight if his own drinking habits were not so well authenticated. As he once admitted: 'I have drunk enough whisky as to make me fit for seizure by the Excise!' And on another occasion he nearly died after a six-week drinking bout in Edinburgh.

Whisky galore!

Hogg, in this respect, was more typical of his age than Burns. As Robert Louis Stevenson was to write: 'There is, in our drunken land, a certain privilege extended to drunkenness. In Scotland, in particular, it is almost respectable, above all when compared with any irregularities between the sexes.' Even in England, hard drinking rarely caused an eyebrow to be raised. Pitt, for example, loaded with hooch, openly vomited behind the Speaker's chair in the House of Commons without incurring the disapproval of his contemporaries. In Victorian times, the Scots consumed four times as much spirits as the English per head of population, and in the previous century things were much worse.

In those days, it was not uncommon for judges to down six bottles of fortified claret or port in an evening (much stronger than today's brands) and it was far from unheard of for hard drinkers, women included, to put two or more bottles of brandy down their necks at a session. At Culloden House, for example, which was the seat of Lord President Forbes, the monthly bill for claret was £40, when the highest price for it was eighteen shillings a dozen bottles. A Montrose laird is on record as rising at ten o'clock, unable to move until he had quaffed a stoup or two of rum or brandy. He generally dined at three, got drunk about four, and retired to bed around five. And at Castle Grant, in the Highlands, attendants remarked disparagingly on the decline in drinking standards evidenced by the fact that some guests actually managed to get to bed on their own two feet!

Funeral fun!

Funerals were invariably drunken riots, their success being reckoned in terms of the number of pates broken. Smollett, in his novel *Humphrey Clinker*, written in 1748, wrote that a Highland gentleman considered it an insult to his family that only 100 gallons of whisky were drunk by mourners at his grandmother's funeral. On more than one occasion, intoxicated revellers lost the corpse before they got to the graveside, and it was rightly remarked that a Scots funeral was more cheerful than an English wedding!

A social historian, the Reverend Henry Graham, wrote: 'It was a dangerous thing to be ill, an expensive thing to die, and often a ruinous thing to be buried.' A good funeral could cost the equivalent of a year's rental. In 1704, it cost £423 sterling to bury Lord Whitelaw, nearly the amount of his salary for two years as a judge. And in 1736, the funeral of the Chief of the Clan Macintosh landed his successors in debts which took nearly a century to clear. The Scottish Parliament, in 1681, tried to curb the extravagance by limiting the number of mourners at a funeral – but the legislation was ignored as hordes of 'mourners', beggars among them, descended on funeral parties for the freeloading. The clergy were indifferent, taking the attitude that they had no further responsibility when the soul of the deceased passed out of their pastoral care!

Most of the French brandy and wines consumed was smuggled, it not being considered improper, even in the most respected circles, to dodge the Exciseman. A Highland laird, Sir Osgood Mackenzie (of whom more later in this chapter), records that it never occurred to him that smuggling was an offence until he was appointed a Justice of the Peace and was obliged to sentence smugglers. Even churches were used, with the clergy conniving, to store illicit liquor. In Dundonald Parish Church, for example, while the faithful intoned their prayers, stocks of hooch reposed in a sanctuary known as 'the smugglers' loft'!

Swing o' the kilt

Now for something else that makes festive occasions go with a swing – the kilt. We've had quite a few inquiries on the subject, the favourite, of course, being whether anything is worn under it. The answer given to us by an Army Master Tailor is 'nothing' except when the soldier takes part in Highland Games or dancing. Rookies, he added, used to be taken aback when, on joining a kilted regiment, they received the order, 'Pants down'! Bet they thought they were getting a chilly reception!

Highland dress was banned after the 1745 rebellion. John Bethune, of Boscombe, Hants, asked us if the law had ever been repealed – or do kilties still run the risk of transportation for seven years? The answer is that the law was relaxed in 1757 and finally repealed by a bill introduced by the Duke of Montrose in 1782, a measure that was passed unopposed.

Several readers have asked how much material is needed to make a Scots kilt. For the real McCoy, with the standard thirty-four pleats, you require about seven yards, single width.

The kilt pin was another subject raised with us. Should it be worn head up or down? And do men wear the pin in the opposite way to women? The pin should, in fact, be worn with the head down at the bottom of the hem – by lads and lassies both.

On with the motley!

Kilts, naturally enough, led us on to the subject of tartans. Mr W. Archibald, of Huntly, Aberdeenshire, asked us if it were true that tartans are comparatively modern, dating only from the Victorian age. We found that a tricky one, since there are widely differing opinions on the subject. For example, John Prebble, author of *Culloden, The Highland Clearances* and other splendid books, believes they were largely produced to satisfy the romantic cravings of Prince Albert, Queen Victoria's consort. Some consider that their origin was inspired by the fertile imagination of Sir Walter Scott, which, if true, would confirm the Victorian date. Others, however, are convinced that tartans, as a distinguishing mark of clans, were created centuries ago.

Finally, we turned to an authoritative work on the subject, *The Tartans of the Clans and Families of Scotland* by the former Lord Lyon King of Arms, Sir Thomas Innes of Learney. His conclusions are that many tartans were, indeed, woven for the first time last century, but that some traditional tartans date back to the eleventh or twelfth century. Sir Thomas pointed out that a clan is simply a group of tribesmen owing allegiance to a Chief or local landowner, and it was natural that each should develop a distinctive dress. Indeed, 'setts', that is, sub-divisions of clans, had coloured fabrics woven for them to distinguish them from the mainstream.

Strictly speaking, a tartan should be worn only by a member of a particular clan – and one tartan is even more restricted than that. It is the Balmoral, which can be worn only by the Royal Family. This tartan of black, red and lavender on a grey background was designed by Prince Albert himself.

'This dear Paradise'

Mention of this tartan takes us on to Balmoral Castle, where, on September 7, 1855, Queen Victoria and Prince Albert took up residence. The castle had been rebuilt on a site by the River Dee, in Aberdeenshire, and the Queen, calling it 'this dear paradise', wrote, 'Everything perfection.' For well over a hundred years now, it has been the 'Highland Home' of the Royal Family, a place for holiday relaxation far from the madding crowds of London and the pomp and ceremony of sovereignty. Queen Victoria adored the Castle, and in fact was criticised for going there so often – a total of seven years sojourn over the rest of her reign.

The faithful servant

The character who dominated many years of Victoria's life until he died at Windsor in March, 1883, aged 56, was, of course, the gillie, John Brown. His role in the history of the times has been the subject of controversy for over a century now, and, as we pen this chapter, there are reports that Dr Michael Macdonald, Curator of the Museum of Scottish Tartans at Comrie, Perthshire, is writing a book in which he suggests that the Queen may have had a son by the gillie.(The Museum, incidentally, has dissociated itself from his researches and conclusions.)

Personally, we'll keep our powder dry until Dr Macdonald fires off in print. Meanwhile, this much information about John Brown is authenticated. He entered the Queen's service permanently in 1851, and in 1858 became her regular attendant out of doors everywhere in the Highlands. In her *Journal* Victoria wrote: 'His attention, care and faithfulness cannot be exceeded.' In December, 1865, promoting him to be her permanent personal attendant, she commented: 'He has all the independence and elevated feelings peculiar to the Highland race, and is singularly straightforward, simple-minded, kind-hearted, and disinterested; always ready to oblige; and of a discretion rarely to be met with.'

By 1860, Brown, who by all accounts was a first-class ghillie, had been enticed into the role of indoor servant. From this period dates the brusque, forthright manner of answering, even advising, the Queen, which so alienated other members of the Royal Family, as well as statesmen and a critical press. No doubt his sedentary occupation also contributed to his early death, since the quantities of whisky he regularly consumed while tramping the hills played havoc with his health in his new post. (Incidentally, the allegedly straight-laced Victoria turned a blind eye to the drunken excesses of her servants. It was the philandering, fun-loving King Edward VII who clamped down on them. One of history's many paradoxes!)

After the death of Albert, Brown became a confidant of the Queen, rather than her servant. Part of the reason, undoubtedly, was that he was no great admirer of rank for rank's sake and had an abrasive wit which the Queen found in amusing contrast to the verbosity of Gladstone, the obsequious flattery of Disraeli, and the servility of some of her courtiers. Another factor is that the happiest days of Victoria's life were spent at Balmoral, and it seems likely that Brown provided a link with the husband she mourned until the day she died. This might explain the envy which Brown aroused and the scandalous gossip which dogged his relationship with the Queen. As Swift remarked more than a century before, 'Those who have no teeth to bite do generally remedy the defect by the foulness of their breath'.

Saviour

John Brown demonstrated his personal courage on at least two occasions when it appeared that the Queen was in danger of being assassinated. The first time, a half-demented Irishman, Arthur O'Connor, approached the Royal coach as it entered Buckingham Palace on February 27, 1872, and put a pistol to the Queen's head. Brown tackled him and disarmed him. As it happened, the pistol was not loaded, but the ex-ghillie wasn't to know that.

On the second occasion, ten years later, a Roderick Maclean fired at the Queen as she dismounted from her train at Windsor to enter her carriage. Again, the faithful servant pounced on the would-be assassin and held him. Maclean was later declared insane – but both incidents did something to mute the criticism of Brown. When he died in 1883, even his most savage critics, such as *Punch,* paid appropriate tribute to him. The Queen was greatly upset, and had a bronze statue erected to him at Balmoral, inscribed:

Friend more than servant,
Loyal, truthful, brave.

After the death of the Queen, the statue and other mementoes were removed.

Victoria is said to have contemplated writing a third volume of her *Journal* on the life of John Brown, but was dissuaded by the Archbishop of Canterbury on the grounds that it might create a public scandal.

What strikes us is that, if the Queen did have an affaire with her one-time gillie, she showed a naivety and lack of commonsense which was not characteristic of her. We'll suspend judgment until the evidence is published!

Tropical plantation

From one Highland estate to another – this time at Inverewe, on the far north-west coast of Scotland. An incredulous reader once asked us if it were true that open-air, tropical gardens can be found north of the border. His scepticism was understandable, but, in fact, sub-tropical gardens flourish at Inverewe, partly due to the benign effects of the Gulf Stream, partly to the genius and application of a remarkable Highland laird, Sir Osgood MacKenzie (1842-1922).

In 1862, Sir Osgood's mother bought him two estates in Wester Ross, one of which – Inverewe – had several miles of coastline. Here he built a house on a rocky peninsula jutting into the sea. The rest of the estate consisted largely of steep braes which could not be cultivated, but there was a narrow strip of land by the shore, which had formerly been a sea-beach. It was here that the famous gardens took shape after years of unremitting labour and inspired craftsmanship. For a start, literally millions of pebbles had to be removed and tons of top-soil brought in from miles away – and brought in by hand-barrows.

A lovesome thing

'A garden is a lovesome thing,' said the poet. But at that time, there were no trees on the Inverewe estate, save dwarf willows, to break the force of the Atlantic winds, often enough gales. Undaunted, the doughty laird planted, initially, Scots firs and other common varieties, then branched out with more unusual types such as Douglas firs, copper beeches, sweet and horse chestnuts, bird cherries, scarlet oaks and the like. Finally followed exotic trees and shrubs which he knew had succeeded in Devon, Cornwall and the west of Ireland. Sir Osgood found, in fact, that some of his experiments came off better than similar ones conducted under glass in the Botanic Gardens at Kew, London.

The laird's next step was to create a fruit and flower garden. He grew raspberries, comice pears, Cox's Orange Pippins and plums, remarking modestly that some of his crops were as luscious as anything to be found in Covent Garden!

Living legend

The Inverewe gardens became a legend in Sir Osgood's

lifetime and, after his death, his daughter, Mrs M. T. Sawyer, added considerably to the collection.

Nowadays, the property is run by the Scottish National Trust and attracts thousands of visitors a year, not merely from this country but from all over the world. New Zealanders have admired the Tree Ferns, Club Palms and Pampas Grass so familiar to them at home; Australians have similarly been astonished to see Eucalyptus trees, some over 90 ft high, and a Eucryphia with a spread of 80 ft; while South Africans can find Kaffir Lillies and other exotic flowers flourishing as in their own land.

In memoriam

Apart from the Inverewe gardens, Sir Osgood left another memorial – a book. At the age of 79, the laird, who was more accustomed to handling a gun or a fishing rod, took up his pen and wrote *A Hundred Years in the Highlands,* a classic of its kind. Based on a manuscript of his uncle, Dr John MacKenzie, and covering the period 1803 to 1860, it is a remarkable record of social history, sport, natural history, horticulture, agriculture, religion, folklore, etc. In his preface, Sir Osgood writes, 'I make no pretence to the art of the writing man,' but the result is a simple, beautifully edited narrative which would be the envy of many a professional scribe.

Since its publication in 1921, the book has run through numerous editions, naturally being extremely popular with homesick Scottish emigres. It is published by Geoffrey Bles, Ltd, 52 Doughty Street, London, but can also be obtained from the National Trust at Inverewe. One reviewer commented: 'A classic autobiography of a Highland laird. Sir Osgood MacKenzie left to the world a garden and a book, and each in its sphere is unique.' We Old Pair are well acquainted with both, and strongly endorse that judgment.

Heroine

Now for a different kind of Flora – Flora Macdonald, the almost legendary heroine who helped Bonnie Prince Charlie to escape after Culloden when the English soldiery were hot on his trail and when only too many Highlanders were willing to betray him for the £30,000 price on his head.

To a reader who asked if there was a memorial to her

anywhere, we said we knew of at least three. One is a stained glass window in St Columba's Church, Portree, Isle of Skye; the second is a Celtic cross in the ancient graveyard of Kilmuir, again Isle of Skye; and the third is a monument in the grounds of Inverness Castle. It portrays her, accompanied by her dog, gazing across the hills to the West Coast. The inscription on it is a quotation from Dr Johnson:

> 'THE PRESERVER OF PRINCE CHARLES
> EDWARD STUART WILL BE MENTIONED
> IN HISTORY, AND IF COURAGE AND
> FIDELITY BE VIRTUES, MENTIONED
> WITH HONOUR.'

The inscription on the Celtic cross is similar.

Incidentally, the popular picture of Flora as a dreamy romantic with Jacobite sympathies is completely false. She wasn't even interested in politics and acted for purely humanitarian motives to save the Prince. She was to remark in later life, 'I have risked my life for both the House of Stuart and the House of Hanover and I cannot see that I am any the better for it.'

Some Burke!

In the summer of 1746, the Prince was in hiding in the Hebridean island of Uist, but as his presence there was suspected, his friends urged him to leave. At the time, Flora was visiting her brother on the island and she was persuaded, if somewhat reluctantly, to smuggle Charles into Skye, disguised as her Irish maid, 'Betty Burke'.

Dressed in a calico gown, a light-coloured quilted petticoat, a mantle of dun camelot with a hood, a cap, broad apron, shoes and stockings, the Prince successfully found temporary asylum at Kingsburgh, Skye.

Mementoes of his sojourn there survived for many years. One was a punch bowl which broke in half as his host tried to wrest it from the bibulous Charles. It was on show at the Inverness Exhibition as late as 1930 when, being carelessly packed, it was smashed to pieces on its return to its owner, a descendant of the Macdonald family.

Among other treasures were the sheets in which Charles slept. One was kept as a shroud for his host's wife; the other for Flora. The room in which he slept was preserved exactly as it was, at least until the time of Dr Johnson's visit there when he lit the Prince's half-burnt candle. Flora parted company with Charles when he sailed for the island of Raasay and eventually a safe, if inglorious, exile.

Flora married Allan Macdonald, son and heir of Macdonald of Kingsburgh, and they emigrated to America where her husband and two sons fought in the War of Independence, holding His Majesty's commissions in the Royal Highland Emigrant Regiment. The family lost nearly everything they possessed, and returned to Skye where Flora died in 1790, bequeathing to her children her two most treasured possessions – a lock of the Prince's hair and a silver shoe-buckle which he had given to her when he changed into the garb of 'Betty Burke'.

Royal launch

Bonnie Prince Charlie launched his royal venture in the summer of 1745, his first step on Scottish soil being on the small island of Eriskay, which lies between Barra and South Uist, on 23 July. The occasion had horticultural, as well as historical, significance.

According to tradition, a rose-pink convolvulus found there grew from seeds which the Prince gathered while he was waiting on the French coast and which dropped from his pocket as he jumped ashore on Eriskay. Certainly the flower is not found elsewhere in the Hebrides.

Charles – at this time disguised as an abbé – found little of the support he had expected but, undeterred, he refused to abandon his venture, declaring to one adviser, 'I am come home, sir, and I will entertain no notion at all of returning to that place from whence I came, for that I am persuaded my faithful Highlanders will stand by me.' In the end, he was proved partly right, and within five months was threatening the Hanoverian throne.

On August 19, 1745, the Royal standard was unfurled at Glenfinnan, at the head of Loch Shiel, where to this day a memorial marks the spot – one of the most desolate but beautiful parts of Scotland, on the road between Fort William and Mallaig.

The rest is history. Charles dragged out a dissipated existence in Rome where, at the end of January, 1788, he died of dropsy and a series of strokes. Betrayed by his wife, Louise, and ignored by the world, he is remembered only in the folk music of the Highlands.

Rotten memory

Another memorial about which we have been asked is the Cumberland Stone – the huge boulder from which William Augustus, Duke of Cumberland and second son of George II, directed the battle of Culloden in 1745. In a brief 25 minutes, the Jacobite forces were decimated by withering cannon and musket fire, the Duke remarking that 'A battle without a cannonade is like a dance without music'.

Apart from his military prowess, 'the Bloody Butcher', as he came to be known, has found two niches in the annals of his time – one musically speaking, the other horticulturally. George Frederick Handel composed *The Conquering Hero* in his honour for a thanksgiving service at St Pauls; and the flower 'Sweet William' was named after him. It was even celebrated in doggerel:

The lily, thistle and the rose
All droop and fade, all die away;
Sweet William only rules the day.
No plant with brighter lustre grows,
Except the laurel on his brows.

The Scots, however, thought the Duke better merited the sobriquet 'Stinking Billy' and named a common weed after him. The Highlanders certainly had no cause to love Cumberland, for what with hangings, transportations and other harsh measures, he largely broke them, the destruction being completed later by those clan leaders who, finding deer and sheep paid better for their pleasures in London, drove their followers into an embittered exile.

Prophetically, the Duke spoke of Loch Ness as 'this diamond in the midst of hell' – prophetically, since he himself contributed largely to the creation of that hell.

Fatal date

A final query on monuments, one concerning a much earlier period of Scottish history. A Suffolk reader, touring Scotland, asked us the significance of a memorial to a king at Kinghorn, Fife. Our LBB had the answer. The king was Alexander III of

Scotland who was killed on March 12, 1286, when his horse fell over a cliff near Kinghorn. Alexander came to the throne in 1249 when he was only eight. Two years later a dynastic marriage was arranged for him with Margaret, eldest daughter of Henry III of England. He made his mark in Scottish history by defeating the Norwegians under Haakon V at Largs in 1263.

Gentlefolk

While we're on kings, here are three other questions concerning them. The first is on the origin of the phrase 'Scotland is a nation of gentlemen'. It was coined by George IV after he had received a loyal welcome on a visit to Scotland in 1822.

The second: Why was David the First of Scotland called 'The Saint'? Because, after he succeeded to the throne in 1124, he established five bishoprics north of the border as well as numerous monasteries for the education of his people. He died in 1153.

And the third: One of our younger readers asked us some years ago how Scotland Yard got its name. The answer is that the original building occupied by the Metropolitan Police from 1828 until 1890 stood on the site of a palace given to Kenneth the Second of Scotland when he came to pay homage to King Edgar about 970. The palace was also used by later Scottish kings.

Lone lake

Next, the lowdown on two lakes. A Hartlepool reader who toured Scotland in the fifties came across the country's only lake but, years later, trying to recollect its name, found that his memory failed him. In fact, it's the Lake of Menteith, some six miles south-west of Callander, Perthshire. It has three islets and on one of them, Inchamahone, there was a priory in which Mary, Queen of Scots, lived from 1547 until 1548.

Another reader queried our answer, referring to a guide book which claimed there were two lakes in Scotland. Curiously, the book didn't specify what they were. However, it is true that there is a second lake, Pressmennan Lake, near Dunbar, in East Lothian. But we discounted it since it is man-made.

Na' leap in the loch, Jock!

Another tourist asked us about the practice of throwing coins into Loch Katrine. She wondered if there was a regular collection of the money as there were thousands of coins in the water. We told her there was no official collection but suggested that enterprising visitors no doubt helped themselves. In fact, the authorities put up notices requesting people not to throw coins into the loch. This is because it is used as a reservoir for Glasgow, and it was feared that folk plunging in at the deep end could cause pollution.

Loch Katrine, incidentally, is the setting of Sir Walter Scott's poem *The Lady of the Lake*. Possibly this explains why people threw money into it – hoping for good luck. Likewise, it was fashionable at one time for passengers on trains crossing the Forth Bridge to hurl cash into the Firth – a deal harder to recover than from Loch Katrine.

Munro's Tables

From lakes and lochs to mountains. What, we were asked, are the Munro Tables? These list Scottish peaks of 3,000 ft or more. They were the brainchild of Sir Hugh Munro, Bart., a native of Angus and founder member of the Scottish Mountaineering Club, of which he was President from 1894 until 1897. In the sixth issue of its *Journal*, his now famous Tables appeared. Sir Hugh listed details of 283 and he personally climbed all but two – the most difficult, 'The Inaccessible Pinnacle of Sgurr Dearg', in Skye, which defeated him several times, and an easy one, Carn Cloich-Mhuillin, in the Cairngorms, which he was leaving to the last. Unfortunately, he died of pneumonia in 1919 before he got round to scaling it.

The 1921 edition of the Tables reduced the number of 3,000 ft peaks to 276 on the grounds that some were approaches to higher ones. In more recent years, three other peaks have been added to the list, and the latest tally we have seen is 279.

The first man to do all the Munros of his day was another President of the Scottish Mountaineering Club, the Reverend A. E. Robertson. It took him eleven years to complete the marathon feat in 1901.

Not English

From time to time we get asked about words which, happily,

are easier to pronounce than the Gaelic names of the mountains mentioned above. The most common is 'Sassenach' which is Gaelic for Saxon, hence Englishman.

And clachan? That's Gaelic for a village or burial place. A village was defined as a place which had a church, inn and smithy.

What of ceilidh? That's a jamboree – a melange of song, dance and story with plenty of grog circulating!

Gralloch? Gaelic word for gutting a deer.

And howtowdie? A Lancashire reader found this one in an old recipe book. It's Scots dialect for a pullet or young chicken.

Still on names, we've been asked what is the most common Scottish one. Despite the claim that all Scots are Jock Tamson's bairns, the right answer is Smith, followed by Brown and Macdonald. Incidentally, there's a suspicion that, in the wake of Culloden, not a few Highland Mac's switched their surnames to the safer nomenclature of Smith or Brown!

Cut to the quick!

Next, two posers on Scottish national matters. The first, put by a Northumberland reader, is: How did the thistle come to be the emblem of Scotland? Legend has it that, in the eighth century, Danish invaders reconnoitring for a night attack on Stirling Castle were creeping around barefooted – but gave themselves away by stumbling on a mass of prickly thistles. They were beaten off and the grateful Scots adopted the humble plant as their emblem.

The other question concerned the Scottish national song, a reader inquiring if it was *Bluebells of Scotland* or *I belong to Glasgow.* The answer is neither. It is *Scots wha hae wi' Wallace bled.* However, in modern times, *Scotland the Brave* seems to have eclipsed it, as anyone who has stood on the terraces of Hampden or Wembley when the Scots take on the auld enemy can testify!

Pre-Darwin

We come now to a handful of Edinburgh characters who have cropped up in correspondence with readers. A Glaswegian once asked us if it were true that a Scotsman hit on the idea of evolution long before Darwin. He vaguely remembered schoolkids chanting a verse about this unacknowledged genius.

There was, in fact, some popular verse about an eccentric eighteenth century judge, Lord Monboddo, though we've been unable to trace the actual words. Monboddo had a high reputation as a judge and as a scholar deeply immersed in the classics and philosophy – and he also dabbled in science of a sort, coming to the conclusion (right in a sense) that human beings were born with tails. No doubt he had in mind the vestigial tail with which they are equipped, but his theory aroused such derision that it was alleged that, whenever a child was born in his household, he would watch at the chamber door in order to see it in its first state, having a notion that the midwives pinched off the infant tails. We'll take that tale with more than a pinch of salt on it!

Monboddo was also ridiculed for his belief in the existence of mermaids and satyrs, and Dr Johnson, who met and enjoyed conversation with him during his Scottish travels, later poked fun at his conviction that the life of the noble savage was superior to that of modern man. Johnson remarked: 'What strange narrowness of mind now is that, to think the things we have not known are better than the things which we have known.' On Boswell retorting, 'Why, Sir, that is a common prejudice,' Johnson commented, 'Yes, sir, but a common prejudice should not be found in one whose trade it is to rectify error.'

Monboddo – who was described as looking like 'an old stuffed monkey in a judge's robes' – is the only one of his profession we have heard of who argued a case of his own in court. He had given a sick horse to a farrier for a specific treatment, but, the animal dying, he sued the man for negligence. He lost the case and is said to have been so incensed with his fellow-judges that he refused to sit on the bench with them and took up his place at the clerks' table!

Despite his eccentricities, Monboddo was highly popular, not least for his supper-parties which were attended by the *literati* of the day and reckoned among the finest in fashionable Edinburgh.

Mirror doesn't lie

The Stair Museum, housed in an ancient mansion on the

Mound, facing Edinburgh's Princes Street, cropped up quite incidentally in another correspondence. We didn't know anything about it at the time but, when we were next in the capital, we looked it up – a delightful place, with mementoes of Burns, Scott and Stevenson. And it was then we came across a book, *Traditions of Edinburgh* by R. Chambers, which contains this extraordinary tale about Lady Stair, who bequeathed her house to the nation.

In her youth, she married a Lord Primrose who turned out to be a monster, forever threatening, sometimes using, violence against her. On one occasion she narrowly escaped with her life by leaping half-dressed from a window as he went to attack her with his sword. Soon afterwards he went abroad and was not heard of for many years. In the meantime, a celebrated fortune-teller came to Edinburgh and, incited by curiosity, Lady Primrose consulted him as to the whereabouts and fate of her husband.

The fortune-teller led her to a large mirror in which she made out the outline of a church wedding and recognised the shadowy bridegroom as her husband. The scene changed, and the priest was about to bid the couple join hands when a stranger burst in, angrily brandishing his sword. She realised it was her brother; upon which the picture dissolved.

Soon after, the brother returned home from a Dutch city and admitted that, on the very day Lady Primrose had consulted the fortune-teller, he had broken up a marriage ceremony in which her husband was about to wed the daughter of a rich man!

Lady Stair's second marriage was much happier, apart from occasions on which her husband drank too much and gave her a beating. Once, when he struck her violently on the face, she sat all night by the sofa on which his Lordship was deep in crapulous slumber, letting her blood and tears flow copiously. In the morning when her husband awoke with alcoholic amnesia, he was full of remorse at his conduct and mended his ways, never drinking more than his beldame permitted!

Lady Stair, who died in November, 1759, had another distinction. She was the first person of breeding in Edinburgh, of her time, to keep a black domestic servant. Negroes had been employed elsewhere long before that, but their status was so low that they were classified in household inventories with goods, clothes and pet birds.

Gallows-bird

The third of our Edinburgh characters was the remarkable Deacon Brodie, a man who moved in good society all his life while staging, unsuspected, a string of burglaries. The ingenious fellow went about with a piece of putty or clay concealed in his palm and took impressions of keys which shopkeepers traditionally hung on a nail at the back of their doors. He was then able to break in during the night and steal what he wanted.

Eventually he was suspected, after a daring robbery on the Excise Office in Canongate, and fled to Amsterdam where he was apprehended and brought back to Edinburgh. After a sojourn in the notorious Old Tolbooth, he was tried, condemned and executed. Even in his dying moments he made history as the first man to demonstrate the excellence of an improvement which he himself had made to the contemporary gibbet. Before him, felons mounted a double ladder and were obliged to jump off it. Deacon Brodie invented 'the drop' and, calmly inspecting his handiwork with an air of undisguised professional approval, was launched into eternity!

Odds and Ends

The final section of this chapter deals with questions which can't be lumped together.

First, what is the largest county in Scotland? Inverness, with 2,695,094 acres.

Has a West Indian ever been recognised as Chief of a Scottish Clan? Yes. In 1959, Langton George Robertson, a 60-year-old Jamaican schoolmaster, was appointed Chief of the Clan Donnachaidh. He was descended from the sixteenth Chief's youngest son who went to Jamaica in 1840.

How many Scots emigrated to South Africa in 1820? We couldn't specify, but there were many among the 4,000 emigrants who sailed from the United Kingdom in that year to Port Elizabeth. Many trekked inland from there to set up homesteads. A memorial marking the historic occasion was erected in Grahamstown in the 1960s.

Gunning for Scots!

In the middle sixties, we settled a controversy triggered off by Alec Vint, of Corby, Northants. He wrote to say his pals believed there was still a law on the Isle of Man allowing inhabitants to shoot a Scotsman on sight! He reckoned this was nonsense – and rightly so. But the hoary old tale does have some foundation in fact. In 1422, the Tynwald, the Manx Parliament, passed a law forbidding Scots to land on the island. This was a measure against raids by Scottish pirates at the time. The Act was repealed in 1697, since when the haggis-bashers have been welcome on Man, kilts, bagpipes and all!

Model Scot!

Years ago, W. Dilley, of Gillingham, Kent, sparked off a lively correspondence about a life-sized wooden figure of a Highlander which then stood outside Catesby's, the famous furniture and lino store in London's Tottenham Court Road. He wanted to know what significance it had. The model was MacPhineas, and legend has it that it got its name from Phineas, an agent during the Jacobite troubles. In the nineteenth century, it stood outside a tobacconist's shop holding snuff in a box from which customers could take a sample pinch.

MacPhineas arrived at Catesby's as part of a consignment of second-hand furniture and, as nobody would buy him, the firm adopted him as an advertising gimmick. A successful one, too, since he hit the headlines annually when students of University College kidnapped him to raise cash for their rag week. Eventually, Catesby's presented the College with a replica.

Other models of Mac were reported in many parts of the country and even abroad – among his haunts being Kennington, Cheltenham, Rotherham, Leeds, Hull, Ipswich, York, Newby, Ripon, and faraway Melbourne.

Short measure

Scots are often accused of being canny with money, but it was only in the 1950s that we Old Pair realised they were giving short measure with their beds. A Buckinghamshire reader, Mr J. Pinchin, of Bletchley, wrote to us, pointing out that whenever he sojourned north of the border he had to sleep curled up because the beds were apparently on the short side. Looking into the matter, we found that Scots manufacturers set the minimum length of a bed at 5ft 9in compared with 6ft 3in in England. But we gather this discrepancy has since been sorted out.

Incidentally, if the Scots were on the mean side with their beds, they made up for it with generous measure of their cot mattresses – 4ft 3in compared with the English 3ft 9in. As we remarked, it seems to prove that the wee bairns of Scotia got a better kick out of life!

Prestigious prestidigitator!

Finally, a tale of an engaging rascal. A few years ago, a friend of one of our readers bought a muzzle-loading shotgun, inscribed 'presented to Walter Scott, Esq. by the Great Wizard of the North'. The reader, Mr W. T. Smith, of Mold, Flintshire, rightly pointed out that Sir Walter Scott presented a gun to a son of his on his fifteenth birthday, but he could not find any reference to 'The Great Wizard'. It was, in fact, a compliment paid to Sir Walter by a literary admirer.

However, the view that the great writer would have inscribed on the gun such an immodest description of himself was challenged by another reader. Not appreciating Scottish self-irony, he came up with an intriguing theory that a magician, one John Henry Anderson, regarded as the Houdini of his age, was the presenter of the gun and the recipient Sir Walter himself. He wrote: 'Anderson performed before Sir Walter Scott in the late 1830s and the poet told him: "They have called me the Wizard of the North, but you are indeed the Great Wizard of the North." ' And from then on, Anderson billed himself as such.

However ingenious that theory, it suffers from major snags. The first is that Anderson could not have performed before Sir Walter in the late 1830s since the writer had died in 1832.

Secondly, it is highly unlikely that Anderson, who was born in 1814 and was only 18 at the time of Sir Walter's death, could have achieved such eminence as to have been invited to perform at Scott's home, Abbotsford.

Thirdly, it is inconceivable that anyone of the time of Scott could possibly have been guilty of an inscription which omitted his title.

PRO par excellence!

Still, the idea aroused our curiosity and we had a look into the career of the remarkable Anderson. Houdini, we found, wrote of him that he was not merely a class magician but also a top-flight self-publicist. He is credited with being the most prolific advertiser of his time and with being the first person to hire sandwich-board men to proclaim his genius as 'Wizard of the North'.

By the 1840s he had made his name and was performing in the best theatres throughout the land, one of his celebrated tricks being 'The Gun Delusion' – no doubt meaning 'The Gun Illusion' – in which he apparently caught a bullet fired from a gun. It's a nice piece of legerdemain not unknown to members of the Magicians' Circle!

Anderson earned a fortune in his heyday, but gave lots away to charity. Yet, however much he may have stored up treasure in Heaven, he seemed to be dogged by a jinx in this life, since three of the theatres of which he took tenancies burnt down. Some coincidence!

The Great Wizard died in Darlington in 1874 and, like rabbits from the proverbial hat, three ladies immediately turned up, all claiming to be his widow and naturally all claiming a stake in his estate. Reckon his final vanishing act was, as usual, superbly timed!

JOKER IN THE PACK

'CARDS,' said a character in Swift's *Polite Conversation*, 'are the devil's books.' If that were the case, then most of us have gone to the devil some of the time and some of us most of the time. By and large, apart from jumping into the deep end of a gambling pool, where you've got to be able to swim well to keep your head above water, you can scarcely indulge in a cheaper or more aimiable and harmless pastime. And, after all, a game of cribbage or whist or what you will makes a change from the goggle box!

We Old Pair have tried our hand not only at cribbage and whist but also solo whist, bridge, poker, pontoon, blackjack (once only for small stakes) and, in our younger days, some of the favourite party games such as cheat, old maid and snap – and, of course, that whiler-away of solitary moments, patience. So we share the interest of readers who have written to us on the subject:

According to Hoyle

The most common question we are asked about cards is: What is the origin of the phrase 'according to Hoyle'? The answer is that Edmund Hoyle is to cards what Newton is to physics – an originator. (We're not suggesting the stature of the two men is comparable!) In Hoyle's case, he set out in his *Short Treatise on Whist*, published in 1742, the rules of the game and how to play it with the best hope of success.

By 1748, it had run to an eighth edition, the latter including chapters on quadrille, piquet and backgammon. A few years later, he put out his final edition – the eleventh – with an additional chapter on chess. Since then, there have been countless editions of his pioneering book published in Britain and America, updated and added to, of course. The last one we consulted (edited by Lawrence H. Dawson) came out in 1972, and had chapters on over eighty games – some increase on the original!

Incidentally, Hoyle was a Londoner, born in 1672, who became a barrister. In middle age, however, having devoted his forensic talents to analysing the odds at the card table, he gave up his practice and lived by teaching whist to the gentry for 'very stiff prices'. He died in Welbeck Street, London, in 1769 at the ripe old age of 97. No doubt, game to the last!

In more recent days, Hoyle is commemorated in the record

Dark Town Poker Club, in which Phil Harris sings, 'We're not playing this game according to Mr Hoyle – we're playing this game according to me!'

And a footnote on Hoyle: we haven't read his original work, but at least one of his precepts on whist has survived the test of time. It is, 'When in doubt, win the trick'.

Starting point

When (a reader asked) was whist introduced to Britain? In the reign of Henry VIII, when it was known as triumph. It was later called 'whisk' and latterly 'whist'. The latter appeal for silence always seems ironic to us in view of the chatter that goes on at whist drives!

Penalty

An avid attender of these drives asked us what the penalty for revoking is. That is when a player, holding one or more of the suit led, plays a card of another suit. The penalty is at the option of the opponents. They can take three tricks from the revoking player and add them to their own tricks, or deduct three points from the offending player's score, or add three points to their own score. The penalty cannot be divided. For example, a player cannot add one or two to his own score and deduct the balance from the revoking side.

Astronomical odds

In March, 1969, Mrs L. Drinkwater, of Burnham-on-Crouch, Essex, wrote to us about a solo whist game in which each of the four players was dealt a complete suit. She rightly reckoned that the odds against this happening must be astronomical. In fact, it is calculated that the chances of one suit alone being dealt to a single player are one in 39,688,347,497 deals. From this fact mathematicians deduce that a deal of four complete suits – a 'perfect' deal, as it is called – should statistically happen only once in 56,000 billion years. Yet we Old Pair have had umpteen reports of its happening. Maybe our readers are unco' lucky!

Solo

We're asked from time to time for the seniority of calls in solo whist. The lowest is 'Prop' and 'Cop' where a player proposes to take eight of the thirteen tricks in partnership with any other player. The card initially turned up determines the trumps.

Solo is the next highest bid. Here a player says he'll attempt to take five or more tricks, with the suit of the turned up card as trumps.

Then comes Misère, where a player intimates that he will attempt to lose all thirteen tricks. There is no trump suit.

After that, there's Abundance where the player will try to take nine tricks, but naming trumps himself.

Abundance in trumps takes precedence. Here a player says he'll take nine or more tricks in the trump suit indicated by the turned up card.

Next, Open Misère, which is the same as ordinary Misère – only after the first trick, the player making the bid must place his remaining twelve cards face up on the table.

Finally, the highest bid is Abundance Declared. This differs from ordinary Abundance in two respects: (a) there is no trump suit; and (b) the lead to the first trick is not made, as in the case of every other declaration, by the player to the dealer's left, but by the caller himself.

Russian whist

A reader asked us what was the origin of the game of bridge, and why it is so called. The game was first played in Turkey by a Russian colony at Istanbul. It was then called Russian whist. It was still so named when introduced to Britain in 1884.

The story of how it came to be known as bridge is a curious one. A couple of families in Leicestershire took to the game and visited each other's house on alternate nights to play it. Their way was over a precarious footbridge, which had no handrail and was often unsafe at night. On leaving after the game, the visiting family would say: 'Thank Heavens, it's your bridge tomorrow night!' And gradually Russian whist came to be known as Russian bridge, and in time 'Russian' was dropped.

Bad end

Our only comment on the above anecdote is that the two families must have been rare friends indeed since, in our experience, bridge frequently brings out the worst in people and, the higher the standard it is played at, the sharper the daggers are drawn. The idea of its being associated with Privilege, Women and Champagne, as Belloc would have us believe, is far-fetched. It can be very cut-throat. One true story sticks in our mind. An American lady (Texan, if we recall aright) was playing with her husband as partner and was getting progressively more annoyed with his hopeless bidding and play. Finally, after a particularly bad opener on his part, she drew a pistol from her handbag and shot him dead. Incidentally, the author of the book on bridge in which we read that account many years ago was a Mr Coffin!

Bad deal

A Manchester reader asked us to settle a dispute about what a 'Yarborough' is. He thought it meant a hand in which you did not hold a single trump. A friend of his maintained that it was a hand in which no card was higher than the nine. The friend was right. This particular hand is named after the second Lord Yarborough who laid odds of 1,000 to one against its occurring. In fact, the odds are actually 1,827 to one against it.

There are many similar bets which can be taken on cards so long as you can work out the odds and so long as you play a sufficiently long sequence of hands. Take, for example, three red cards and three black, shuffle them and lay them out face down. Ask an opponent to draw any three. His only possibilities are that he will draw three reds, or two reds and a black, or one red and two blacks, or three blacks. Your opponent might think he was on to a good thing if you offered him three to one that he will draw two cards of one colour, the third of the other colour.

Not a chance! At least not a chance over a period of time. The chances of drawing two of one colour and one of another are nine out of ten – so the genuine odds offered should be not less than nine to one.

Top of the pops

A question that cropped up some time ago was: 'What is the most popular card game in Britain?' Cribbage, followed by solo whist. In the United States, it's stud poker.

Here are some of the questions we've been asked about cribbage. Can the game be won simply by the turn-up card being a Jack and thus scoring two for 'his heels'?

Yes, unless there is a previous agreement to ban this. There's nothing in the rules to forbid it.

An Ellesmere Port, Cheshire, reader disputed a friend's claim that the dealer must peg at least one. The friend was right. The rule book states: 'The dealer is sure to peg at least one point in every hand, for he will have a "go" on the last card, if not earlier.'

Flush

Another reader, from Felbridge, Surrey, who had played cribbage for fifty years wrote to us in 1975 to ask if there was such a thing in that game as a flush. He was convinced there wasn't. As it happens, he was mistaken. Four cards of the same suit in the hand count four, and if the starter, or turn-up card, is also of the suit, that's another one. For the box, or crib, however, all four cards must be of the same suit as the turn-up, and count five. As we commented at the time, our reader must have lost many a peg over the years!

Impossible

The maximum possible score for one hand in cribbage is 29. But what, asked one reader, are the impossible scores? No hand can make a count of 19, 25, 26 or 27.

What, asked another reader, from Newport, Gwent, who had seen the maximum 29 scored on one hand, are the odds against it? They are 216,579 to one.

Morgan's Orchard

Many readers have been puzzled by the origin of this phrase, and its application. We Old Codgers have never come to any positive conclusion. It can, and commonly does, apply to a pair of fours. But some players use it in reference to any two pairs or even to a single four.

Various explanations canvassed by readers are:

(a) it's a corruption of 'Morgan's Horses', an expression derived from the United States when teams of four horses were known as 'Morgans' – and so applied to any four in hand.

(b) Poker players use the same term for the number nine card. They claim that a legendary poker expert, Morgan, had a speech defect which caused him to say 'tree trees' instead of 'three threes' – hence the orchard. (If he'd been an Oirishman, we might have swallowed that one!)

(c) Morgan, first name Bill, according to another explanation, was landlord of the Robin Hood pub in Alfreton, Derbyshire, in Edwardian days. At the back of the tavern was a garden in which only a pear tree survived. If a crib player had only a pair in his hand and a pair in the box, he'd say 'Morgan's Orchard' – all pears and nothing else.

(d) A similar explanation came from a Cheadle Hume, Cheshire, reader, whose version was that a Tom Morgan had a fine orchard which was raided one night and only two rotten pears were left.

Like the raiders, take your pick of that lot!

Ragged

A final question on cribbage: What cards constitute a 'ragged thirteen'? Two aces, six, seven and eight – scoring fifteen 8, 2 for a pair, and 3 for a run. Total 13.

Poker odds

Now some questions on the odds of getting various hands in poker. First, we were asked: 'Which is higher – a full house or a flush? A full house, because in a 52 card deck there are only 3,744 possible full houses compared with 5,108 possible flushes.

What are the odds against getting a run? 254 to one.

What are the chances of getting four cards of a kind? They are 4,164 to one.

What is the total number of possible hands in poker? In a 52 card deck, 2,598,960.

If a poker player holds an eight, a nine, a jack and a queen, what are the odds of drawing a ten of any suit to complete the run? 11 to one.

A reader from Port Sunlight, Cheshire, told us that in 1971 he was dealt the Ace, King, Queen, Jack and Ten of Hearts, and he wanted to know the odds against this. Using a full pack, a mere 649,739 to one.

Precedence

One argument we were called on to settle was in a Durham pub, where the issue was: Does a flush of any five clubs or five hearts beat a full house of any three of a kind and any pair? No. Any full house beats any flush, except a straight flush, of course.

Another question: Which is the highest Royal Flush in poker – spades, hearts, etc? None has precedence, so two hands which are identical, card for card, are equal.

Terms

Three questions now on terms used in poker: What is a Big Tiger? A king high, eight low hand without a pair in it.

What are the terms for three cards, and four cards, of a kind? The former is a prial, the latter a mournival. Prial is a contraction of pair-royal.

And where does the word 'jackpot' come from? From draw-poker. It's a pool or 'pot' in which the betting can't start until one player has opened with at least a pair of jacks or better. If no player can open, then all must 'ante-up' – put in their original stake again – and the cards are re-dealt. In this way the jackpot is built up until somebody can open the game.

Murder most foul

In the first volume of excerpts from our Little Black Book, we dealt with the question of what a 'Dead Man's Hand' is in poker. But as the book has been out of print for some years, and the query keeps cropping up, we'll summarise what we said then.

'Dead Man's Hand' was the poker hand held by Wild Bill Hickok when he was shot dead in a saloon at Deadwood, Dakota Territory, on August 2, 1876. It consisted of two pairs, Aces and Eights, in Spades and Clubs, with either the Jack of Diamonds or the Queen of Hearts as his fifth card.

Legend had it that Hickok caught a gambler, Jack McCall, cheating and ordered him out of town. But McCall sneaked back and murdered the Marshal. In fact, at his trial McCall admitted that he had been bribed to kill Wild Bill. He was hanged.

Incidentally, another myth is that Wild Bill was one of the 'fastest guns' in the West, credited with killing 85 men. In fact, his tally was seven, shot out of provocation or in the course of his duties as a law officer.

Pontoon

Curiously enough, although pontoon is a highly popular

game, we hardly ever receive any inquiries about it. One standard question concerns the origin of the name. It is simply a corruption of the French 'vingt-un' (twenty-one) brought back to Britain last century by troops who had fought on the Continent.

Another point raised by a reader was: 'Why is pontoon not allowed in British casinos?' This is because the banker's edge is more than the Gaming Board will sanction, namely, that if a player and the bank both have the same score, the bank wins. By contrast, in blackjack, when the punter's score is the same as the banker's, no stakes are won or lost. This is known as 'stand-off'.

Pontoon, incidentally, is legal in Isle of Man casinos.

Skill and luck

Here's an odd bit of observation which, we admit, hadn't occurred to us until we came upon it in a book on gambling. There is only one card game which depends on 100 per cent skill and one which relies on 100 per cent luck. Got it worked out? The former is snap, the latter beggar-my-neighbour.

Good advice

The same book contains many pearls of wisdom. One is: 'The law of conservation of wealth ensures that capital is attracted from the poorer to the richer when hazarded on chance.' Hence the inequitable odds offered by bookmakers, casino operators and other promoters.

Another bit of advice for the amateur gambler having a minor flutter is to compete against the crowd. Thus, in filling in a football coupon, start at the bottom as most people take their selections from the top. And in betting on horses, choose those with a chance but ridden by less well-known jockeys or possessing drab names (women punters, in particular, tend to go for fancy names!).

Makes sense, really, and talking of odds against the better puts us in mind of another topic – how the odds are crookedly stacked against the card player. 'There be those that can pack the cards and cannot play,' says Bacon. But there are also those who can stack them and play only too well. We've had no first experience of being rooked ourselves, but a book we came across some years ago explained some of the techniques used by professional cheats. Quite an eye-opener it was!

Peek-a-boo!

We had admittedly been aware of minor cheating at cards – peeking at an opponent's hand, signalling to one's partner, etc., all innocent enough at a friendly whist drive or bridge party where the stakes are minimal. But we hadn't a glimmering of the sophisticated techniques used by professional sharpers when the chips are really down, until we consulted this book, *How to Cheat at Cards*, by A. D. Livingston (MacMillan).

Take peeking, for example. The expert can read cards in advance by a variety of techniques, bulging the top card, moving the others fractionally aside and even, while dealing one card, peeking at the next.

The art was brought to perfection by an American card detective, Michael MacDougall, who proved that he could take an honestly shuffled and cut pack and deal a hand in which all the high cards fall to himself and his partner. He 'flashes' a card by holding it not more than a thirty-second of an inch apart from the others – enough for his practised eye to detect what the card is by a glimpse of its corner. He then deals it to an opponent if it is a low card or saves it for himself or his partner if it is a high one. It is a skill which only a top-class magician can master.

On one occasion, MacDougall demonstrated his genius in front of 100 bridge experts. The pack was shuffled and cut independently, yet before the first hand was even dealt, MacDougall bid six no trump – and made them!

Other peeking techniques involve the use of reflectors to get a look at the underside of cards. These can be very tiny and placed in a pipe, a ring, even a cigarette. One sharper used a sliver of glass under a fingernail. But professionals apparently used to prefer having a shiny object positioned on a table, a cigarette case, a money clip or an ashtray, for example.

A nice story is told of a gambler in South Dakota who posed as a gold prospector and who, when he hit town, unsheathed a knife with a shiny blade, put it on the table, and threatened to stick it in anyone he caught cheating. The knife stayed put as the gambler, Cactus Pete, was the only sharper sitting in.

Markers

Another method of cheating is to mark cards. This can be done in a variety of ways – by slight bending of high ones, by pin pricks in a particular corner, by cutting a minute sliver from low cards, making the high ones easily identifiable to a sharper ('belly-stripping' as it is called). No good for us Old Codgers! Our eyesight and reactions wouldn't be nearly fast enough even if we were inclined to win a few coppers at cribbage or gin rummy.

Signal corps

Signalling is another common form of cheating. Messages can be passed between partners on a pre-arranged code of movements, how the cards are held, a fractional difference in tone of voice, a clearing of the throat, etc. Or a player can make use of a kibitzer. That is a person who has asked for, and received, permission to watch a game. He can communicate information by eye signals, etc.

Accused

In 1965, during the World Bridge Championships at Buenos Aires, the British experts, Terence Reese and Boris Schapiro, were accused of using finger signals. They were eventually cleared, and wrote a book about their experience called *Story of an Accusation* which illustrates the difficulty of either proving or disproving allegations of this type of cheating.

Reese makes the point that finger signals are crude and easily detected, while Schapiro, at one point in the book, says it is easy to cheat at bridge without being found out.

In that case, and considering that in the United States alone a billion dollars a year are staked on the game, why do professional gamblers tend to ignore it? Two reasons. The first is that the game is too slow for them to use the full range of their dirty tricks. The second is that bridge is essentially a game of skill in which better players must win over a period of time. If the results don't conform to their judgment of what they should be, they naturally smell a rat. Anyway, they develop a sixth sense for detecting signals.

The bridge master, Ely Culbertson, records that, in London, he was once the victim of the smartest signalling system he had ever encountered. It consisted of precise timing during bidding and play, based on the number of seconds which elapsed before a bid or a play was made. The length of each period of silence indicated strength or weakness in a particular suit. It took him a few rubbers to rumble the rascals. Finally, after listening to one silent count, he rose, continuing loudly, 'eight, nine, etc. . . . that knocks me out, gentlemen. Good-bye.'

Outplayed

It was Culbertson, incidentally, who devised the trap hands which James Bond, in Ian Fleming's novel *Moonraker*, used to outwit the arch-villain Drax. Ely, of course, was merely teaching pupils about the dangers of being overconfident; Bond was out to teach Drax another kind of lesson. An expensive one, too. The hands are as follows:

	Bond	
	S. Nil.	
	H. Nil.	
	D. Q,8,7,6,5,4,3,2.	
	C. A,Q,10,8,4.	
Drax		*Meyer*
S. A,K,Q,J.		S. 6,5,4,3,2.
H. A,K,Q,J.		H. 10,9,8,7,2.
D. A,K.		D. J,10,9.
C. K,J,9.		C. Nil.
	M.	
	S. 10,9,8,7.	
	H. 6,5,4,3.	
	D. Nil.	
	C. 7,6,5,3,2.	

Bond has fixed a deck identical to one of those in play, and switches them by a bit of sleight of hand. Drax, naturally enough, thinks he holds a 'rock-crusher' but learns to his cost that Bond has a lay down Grand Slam. With doubles, redoubles and side bets, the villain loses about £15,000! Don't reckon he went much on the Bard's crack about 'the game's thing . . .'

Chinese puzzle

To get back to straight dealing, a question we've been asked several times is: 'Who invented playing cards?' The Chinese claim to have done so in the reign of S'eun-Ho in AD 1120 for the added entertainment of his concubines. But how they got to Europe after a lapse of well over two hundred years remains a mystery.

First mention of them is in a treatise published in Italy in 1377, and from the start their popularity was assured. They received a considerable plug in 1423, when a Franciscan friar, St Bernard of Siena, preached a famous sermon in Bologna in which he called them 'the invention of the devil'.

From Italy, card playing spread to Germany and France and, in the early fifteenth century, to England. By 1450, a thriving home industry had been established and, to protect it, Edward IV issued a Statute in the third year of his reign (1463-64) prohibiting the import of 'Cardes a Juer' (playing cards). In little over half-a-century, gambling and gaming were so rife that an attempt was made to curb them by the Proclamation of May, 1526. But the yeomen of merrie England weren't having any of it and accused Cardinal Wolsey of being, mean-spiritedly, behind the clampdown, remarking that he 'grudged every manne's pleasure savying his own'. The Proclamation was soon forgotten.

For the next three centuries cards were produced by stencil or laboriously hand painted. But in 1832, Thomas de la Rue was granted letters patent to revolutionise playing cards by producing them in true colour printing with a high gloss finish. He is, in short, the father of the modern playing card.

In recent years, some 60,000,000 to 70,000,000 decks are sold annually throughout the world. In the United Kingdom alone, the figure varies between 5,000,000 and 11,000,000.

Price on a pack

Why, asked a Peterborough reader, is the Ace of Spades printed larger than the other three Aces? The most probable reason is that, when excise duty was first payable on playing cards, the Customs stamp was put on the Ace of Spades, which was printed larger for that purpose. Since then, the card has been used as the trade mark of the manufacturer.

Duty was introduced in 1750 at five bob a gross of packs, but went up to 2s 6d a single pack in 1789. In 1862, it was cut to 3d, remaining at that rate until it was abolished in August, 1960.

Incidentally, on the subject of aces, we've been asked what is the origin of the word. It is the Latin 'as', meaning 'a unit' or 'one'.

Pip, pip, pip, pip . . .

And the question of units brings us to a supplementary from a Manchester reader. He asked if it were true that a pack of playing cards contains 365 pips. Yes. But only if you count a knave as eleven, a queen as twelve, a king as thirteen, and the Joker as one.

Just as these pips add up to the number of days in a year, so there are fifty-two cards in a pack, as weeks for the year, four suits matching the four seasons; and thirteen cards in each suit, as there are thirteen weeks in each quarter of the year. Rummy, eh!

Queens in mourning

Two more historical questions. Is it a fact that 'queens' were once banned from packs of cards? Indeed they were. They were temporarily withdrawn as a mark of respect on the death of Caroline, wife of George the Second, in 1737.

And going further back, to what period do the costumes of the king, queen and knave belong? To the reign of Henry VIII. The King of Clubs is said to represent the Pope; Spades, the King of France; and Hearts, the King of England, that is Henry himself.

Fortune tellers

There are two types of pack – the Tarot, or Major Arcana, and the Minor Arcana. The present day pack is derived from the latter, though originally it consisted of fifty-six cards. This was reduced to fifty-two by dropping the four knights. The present suits – spades, hearts, diamonds, clubs – used to be coins, cups, swords and staffs, representing commerce, spirituality, war and agriculture.

The Tarot pack consisted of twenty-two pictorial cards, none of which is obviously related to the others. Its origin is a mystery. All that is known is that Tarot cards were used in Europe as early as the fourteenth century. From the start, they were employed not only for gaming but also for fortune telling. The same applied to the Minor Arcana packs.

Over the centuries, cartomancy (to give fortune telling by cards its technical name) became a vogue. Whether the practitioners were simply psychologically shrewd, psychic or merely charlatans is a matter for individual judgment. Certainly, in France, two of them at least made considerable fortunes out of their talents. The first was a rascal who reversed the spelling of his name and called himself 'Etteilla'. He flourished about 1775.

The other, and more famous, name was that of Mademoiselle Lenormand, who was a society success at the time of the French Revolution and the Napoleonic Wars. She was consulted by Napoleon himself – and, indeed, was twice flung into jail for predictions that ran counter to his plans – and she was an intimate of the Empress Josephine. She is also said to have read the fortune of Robespierre, Danton, Talleyrand and others.

According to Dennis Wheatley (in his book *The Devil and All His Works*), she gave a reading to Marshal Murat, King of Naples, who cut the unlucky King of Diamonds four times in succession. When he refused to accept her interpretation, she flung the cards at him and said he would either be hanged or shot while in captivity. He was executed by firing squad in 1815.

The fateful twenty-two

For the record, the Tarot cards, which symbolise all aspects of temporal and spiritual life, are as follows:

The Juggler represents the will of God, the Creation and the quickening of life.
The High Priestess represents duality and virginity.
The Empress represents beauty and pregnancy.
The Emperor represents material things and worldly authority.
The Pope represents spiritual power.
The Lovers represent innocence, love and the union of opposites.
The Chariot represents exaltation and the passage of the spirit towards beatitude.
Justice represents the achievement of equilibrium.
The Hermit represents puberty and hidden light.

The Wheel of Fortune represents the path towards one's destiny.
Strength represents the discipline that leads to ecstasy.
The Hanged Man represents the release of the waters of life.
Death represents resurrection.
Temperance represents change and transformation.
The Devil represents the dominance of pride, ambition and lust.
The Tower Struck by Lightning represents collapse, violence and destruction, imprisonment or death.
The Star represents intuition, hope and bliss.
The Moon represents the breaking of the hymen and also the darkness of the womb.
The Sun represents the light of true intelligence.
The Day of Judgment represents aspiration towards higher things.
The World represents joy, and release from earthly existence.
The last card, the Fool, corresponds to O, which contains all qualities yet has none; and it represents divine madness.

Unlucky for some

We Old Pair don't dabble in matters arcane, so we have to take other people's word for it that, of the four suits, hearts and clubs are considered lucky, spades and diamonds unlucky. As we pointed out above, Marshal Murat came to a sticky end after the King of Diamonds turned up four times in succession. And Napoleon swore that his unluckiest card was the Eight of Spades. Others have found ill omens in the Ace and Queen of Spades, particularly when they turn up one after the other. Here are two accounts of misfortune where the two cards played a fateful part. One is fictional, the other, regrettably, all too true.

The Russian author, Pushkin, provides the first with a psychological and supernatural short story, *The Queen of Spades*, which is one of the classics of Western European literature.

Briefly, the plot is that a German, commissioned in a Russian regiment, hears of an ancient Countess who possesses the secret of how to make a fortune at gaming. She knows the sequence of three cards which, betted on in the right order, will infallibly beat the bank. Hermann, as he is called, was not a gambler but he became obsessed by the story and eventually obtained an audience with the Countess. He asked for her secret; she refused. Losing his temper he brandished his revolver; she died of fright.

The grave's secret

A few days later, Hermann is awakened from a half-drunk slumber to find a white figure in his bedroom. It is the Countess. She says: 'I have come to you against my will, but I have been commanded to grant you your request. The three, seven and ace are the winning cards. Only you must never stake more than one at a time and never play again in your life.'

For three nights running, Hermann goes to a wealthy gambler's house. On the first night he stakes all his money on the three, and wins. The next night he stakes his original money plus his winnings on the seven. Again he wins. With his money redoubled, he returns the third night, convinced that he will turn up the ace and again beat the bank. Two cards are dealt. Hermann turns up the Queen of Spades who (he observes) looks remarkably like the dead Countess. The bank turns up the Ace of Spades and collects. Hermann is ruined and goes mad.

Omen in the cards

So much for the fictional. The factual concerns the water speed king, Donald Campbell, who was killed on Coniston Water, in the Lake District, on January 4, 1967.

The night before his death in Bluebird, as he made his final, ill-fated attempt on the world speed record, Campbell, who was notoriously superstitious, was playing Russian patience, a game he had learnt in Las Vegas.

Apparently, the unluckiest combination you can turn up in this game is the Ace of Spades and the Queen of Spades (as in Pushkin's tale). Campbell turned it up, the Ace first, then the Queen. Deeply depressed, he remarked that Mary, Queen of Scots, had turned up the same combination and regarded it as an omen that she would be beheaded. He added: 'One of my family is going to get the chop. I pray to God it isn't me.'

He sent for another pack of cards – only to find that it was green-backed, and green was a colour he considered unlucky. He wouldn't drive a green car, and he wouldn't, if he could avoid it, make a trial run on the 13th of the month. So the next day, even though it wasn't the 13th, he went to his death, convinced that it was inevitable.

Old wives' tales . . . or?

Some may shrug such superstitions aside. For example, Professor John Cohen, an eminent psychologist at Manchester University, has said: 'People like Donald Campbell are dealing with danger that can be beyond their control. Natural human weakness makes them clutch at straws in the hope that they will invoke the help of the supernatural.'

However, in the book we have mentioned above, Dennis Wheatley records that on one occasion, when playing with a Tarot pack, he twice cut the Tower Struck by Lightning, in each case the card being upside down. This presages financial loss and possible imprisonment. At the time, he was a well-off wine merchant and had no reason to anticipate trouble. But a year later, the slump of 1929 reduced him to near bankruptcy. He was also accused of fraud and, but for a good accountant who completely cleared his name, might have gone to prison. After that, he never pooh-poohed the Tarot cards!

Ill-fated

While we're on the subject of ill-fortune, here are two questions about cards reputed to be associated with bad luck.

Which card in the pack, asked a reader, is known as 'The Devil's Bed Posts'? And why? The card is the Four of Clubs. It was said to be of ill-omen in the days of four-posters!

A final query, which crops up quite often: Why is the nine of diamonds called 'The curse of Scotland'? We dealt with this one in the first volume of our Little Black Book, but our explanation has been challenged by several readers, two of whom have come up with theories at least as plausible as that which we plumped for. Here are all three—

We said the curse probably had its origin in the heraldic arms of James Dalrymple, first Earl of Stair. The first quarter of his shield showed nine diamonds – or 'lozenges' – on a St Andrews Cross. Dalrymple was considered the 'Curse of

Scotland' for his part in the Massacre of Glencoe in 1692, and sponsorship of the Union with England in 1707.

However, John Pennington, from Castleford, Yorkshire, suggested the origin of the phrase is in an ancient card game called 'Pope Joan'. This game was named after a mythical woman Pope of the ninth century and in it the Nine of Diamonds is 'the Pope'. Scottish Protestants, perhaps, referred to the card as 'The Curse of Scotland' because of their extreme antipathy to Roman Catholicism.

Another explanation came from Mrs Winnie Whiteman, of Coventry. She suggested that 'curse' is a corruption of 'cross'. In early playing cards the Nine of Diamonds was designed diagonally like a St Andrew's cross – the cross of Scotland.

All plausible theories from which to take your pick! And with that, we'll have another rifle through our LBB and see what we can deal for the next chapter.

NOBLE ARTISTES

READER, have you ever seen a fight? If not, you have a pleasure to come, at least if it is a fight like that between the Gas-man and Bill Neate.

No, those aren't our words – they are from that literary classic, *The Fight*, by critic and essayist William Hazlitt in which he gives a fascinating account of a bare-knuckle contest between Tom Hickman, the Gas-man, and Bill Neate, the Bristol Bull, on December 11, 1821.

Probably few of Hazlitt's readers ever did see a fight, for the sport was illegal in those days and most bouts took place in the country, out of the law's way – Hazlitt himself had to take two stage coaches from London to Newbury and then walk nine miles to the scene of the fight, near Hungerford, Berks.

On the other hand, most of our readers probably have seen a fight, if only through the medium of television, but we doubt if there is any still alive who witnessed one of the classic encounters between the old-style prize-fighters as described by Hazlitt. Though we did once publish a letter from an old gent who, as a thirteen-year-old, saw a bare-fist bout in his home town of Hull:

'They slugged away at each other,' reported our reader, 'until both could hardly stand. At the finish they were so bloody that they might have just come out of a butcher's shop. What shook my pal and me was that we found out the boxers were brothers!'

We hope that gent is reading this. If so, he will be ninety-five. Yet despite their remoteness in time – or possibly because of it – the great days of pugilism have a fascination and glamour which still provoke argument and reminiscence, so that even now we Old Pair are sometimes called upon to referee in matters of bare fisticuffs.

We don't propose to give a blow by blow account of all the fights, merely some of the highlights that have been recorded in the Live Letters column, plus some background information on the worthies of the prize-ring.

Artful Figg

'The noble art of self defence' is a familiar definition of boxing, but when we were asked who coined the phrase we found ourselves staggering in the first round. The earliest reference we could find was the business card of James Figg, acknowledged the first heavyweight champion of England in 1719. The card, designed by Figg's friend William Hogarth, the great artist and cartoonist, who also painted a portrait of the champ, proclaimed: 'James Figg, Master of ye Noble Science of Defence on ye right hand in Oxford Road near Adam & Eve court teaches Gentlemen ye use of ye small backsword and quarterstaff at home & abroad.'

But did Figg originate the phrase? It seems unlikely, but not impossible. Whoever the author was, as applied to the early prizefighters the definition was incongruous, to say the least, for their history is one of protracted savage bouts which often resulted in maiming and sometimes death.

As his advertising card indicated, Figg, born in Thame, Oxon, in 1695, was originally an expert with the broadsword and cudgel. In the first of his three fights with his chief challenger, Ned Sutton, a pipe-maker from Gravesend, the contestants started with cudgels before continuing with their fists! Figg retired undefeated in 1730, but died, aged thirty-nine, four years later.

Boxer's corner

Figg's successor as champ was one of his pupils, George Taylor, who had opened a boxing booth in Tottenham Court Road and it was in his own booth, some time between 1735 and 1740, that Taylor lost his title.

We were 'introduced' to the chap who took it from him by a reader who thought to catch us out with the question: Which ex-boxing champion is buried in Westminster Abbey? Not to be floored by what we suspected was a low blow, we sent our lad George to the Abbey where he searched for some hours in vain. Then, in the West Cloister, he found the very bloke under his feet – Jack Broughton, born in Gloucestershire in 1704, and another of Figg's proteges.

It was Broughton, rather than his mentor, who developed boxing into an art. Before him, a prize-fight was usually no more than a toe-to-toe slugging match. 'Gentleman Jack' introduced footwork, parrying, attacking and retreating. Like Figg, he had a private boxing school, in Hanway Street, off London's Tottenham Court Road, where he gave lessons to the sons of the gentry and it was to save the aristocratic looks of his customers that Broughton invented boxing gloves – he called them 'mufflers' – though for sparring only.

Killer puncher

Not that Broughton pulled his punches when in the actual prize ring. He took Taylor's title in a hectic bout which lasted only twenty minutes. And in 1741, over forty-five minutes he handed out such a savage beating to George Stevenson, the Fighting Coachman, that the poor chap died a month later.

Apparently it was this tragedy which caused Broughton to draw up the first rules of boxing. 'As agreed by several gentlemen at Broughton's Ampitheatre, Tottenham Court Road, August 16, 1743', the most important of these rules were that a man should not be hit when he was down and that if a man were unable to come up to the yard-wide starting point within half a minute after a fall, he should be deemed beaten. Incidentally, until the Marquess of Queensberry Rules of 1866, there was no time limit on a round, it continued until one man fell.

Broughton's Rules, which earned him the soubriquet of the Father of Boxing, governed the sport until 1838, when the London Prize Ring Rules were introduced by the British Pugilists' Protective Association.

In the meantime, our Jack had come under the patronage of the Duke of Cumberland, third son of George II and later notorious as the 'Butcher of Culloden'. The Duke secured for him a post as a Yeoman of the Guard. Their happy relationship came to an end on April 10, 1750, when Broughton defended his title against Jack Slack, grandson of Figg. Admittedly the champion was forty-six, and Slack, a Norwich butcher and hence dubbed the 'Knight of the Cleaver', was several years younger and had won several bouts in short order. But only three months previously, Slack had been knocked out in twenty-five minutes by George Taylor, the man Broughton had taken the title from more than ten years earlier.

Bad loser

So the Duke had enough confidence in his champion to back him to the tune of £10,000. Perhaps Broughton had too much confidence in himself, for Slack whipped him in fourteen minutes. Understandably, the Duke was mightily displeased and turned nasty on his former favourite, but Broughton had looked after his prize monies and lived comfortably to the age of eighty-five. He had become a verger of Westminster Abbey and, as a dying wish, was buried there in 1789.

Slack held the championship for ten years and during his reign beat the first French pugilist of note, a 6ft 6ins, 16st giant allegedly named Monsieur Petit! Then on June 17, 1760, he lost the title to Bill Stevens, 'The Nailer'. Alas for the Duke of Cumberland, he again backed the wrong man and lost another small fortune. His Grace swore that Slack had sold the fight. He may well have been right, for the Norwich butcher was reputed to be not above taking a dive and after losing to Stevens he himself promoted a match between the new champ and one George Meggs. The latter won, Stevens having been bought off and Slack receiving fifty guineas from Meggs for the arrangement.

Handicapped champ

For the next twenty or so years the boxing game was in a poor state, with the 'title' changing hands in a series of unsatisfactory and often unsavoury bouts. Then from 1783 to 1791 England at last had a champion worthy of the name, Tom Johnson, who defended, his title honestly against all comers. But even he eventually lost the title in an anti-climatic manner. Matched against Benjamin 'Big Ben' Brain at Wrotham, Kent, on January 17, 1791, the champion smashed his right hand against a ring post early in the fight and was beaten in twenty-one minutes. Brain never defended his title. Three years later he was matched with Will Wood but was taken suddenly ill with a liver complaint before the fight and died on April 8, 1794, aged forty-one.

Desperate Dan

But the next boxer to develop the noble art from the stage to which Jack Broughton had brought it (no pun intended) thirty-odd years earlier was an English-Spanish Jew. We mentioned him in Live Letters as the result of an enquiry from a reader who remembered that his grandfather, apparently a boxing fan, had had a bulldog which he named 'Mendoza' after a famous barefist fighter. Did we know anything about him?

We did. Daniel Mendoza was born in Aldgate, of English and Spanish parents, in 1764. At the age of twenty he won his first big fight, in Mile End, against one Harry the Coalheaver, but Daniel himself suffered heavy damage in the forty-minute battle. Compared with most pugilists of that time, Mendoza was a little 'un, standing 5ft 7in and weighing less than 11½st, hardly more than a middleweight, in fact. So he concentrated on developing a defensive style based on fast footwork and a straight left. And these tactics paid off, with a series of impressive victories over larger, though cruder, opponents. Admittedly, some members of the Fancy, as barefist fight fans were known, considered this scientific, evasive technique unsporting compared to the more usual blow-for-blow roughhousing style – a criticism sometimes levelled at another great champion, Muhammad Ali, nearly two hundred years later.

But there was no denying its effectiveness. Mendoza had some thirty-five fights, an unusually large number for those days, evidence of his skill in avoiding punishment.

Bitter rivals

There were two notable defeats. The first was against Richard Humphries, then considered the best heavyweight around. This seems to have been something of a grudge match. Mendoza had taken only twenty minutes to finish off Sam Martin, the Bath Butcher, a man who had gone 105 minutes with Humphries. And Mendoza, who was to see the inside of a debtors' prison more than once, owed Humphries money. They met to settle scores at Odiham, Hants, on January 9, 1788. After twenty-nine minutes Mendoza was struck down, twisted his leg and was unable to continue.

But it had been such a good match that a return was inevitable. It took place at Stilton, Hunts, on May 6, 1789, and this time Mendoza's skill prevailed from the start, scoring the first three knock-downs. Nevertheless the fight went on for fifty-two minutes, when Humphries fell without being hit, which under the rules of the time, gave Mendoza victory.

They met for a third time, on September 29, 1790, when Mendoza confirmed his superiority by stopping Humphries in only fifteen minutes. Daniel clinched his right to Ben Brain's undefended title by defeating Squire Fitzgerald, the pride of Ireland (Mendoza subsequently influenced the development of boxing in Ireland through exhibitions there) and by twice stopping Bill Warr, a rival claimant, in 1792 and 1794.

Long-haired loser

His reign ended on April 15, 1795, when he accepted a challenge from Gentleman John Jackson. The challenger had been retired from the ring for six years, having broken a leg in a fight with George Ingleston, 'The Brewer', but he was only twenty-six and the champion was now thirty-two. Furthermore, Mendoza entered the ring with his hair worn long and 'Gentleman' or not, Jackson took advantage of this, holding his opponent by his locks while punching him with the other hand. But it was within the rules at the time and Mendoza succumbed after only eleven minutes of actual fighting.

Thereafter boxers took the precaution of having their hair cut before fights.

Mendoza's fortunes seem to have fluctuated after that defeat. At various times he ran a successful boxing school, kept a pub in Whitechapel and was even proprietor of the Lyceum in the Strand – no doubt it became a Mecca for boxing fans! Yet there was recurring trouble with money, which resulted in at least three spells in prison.

Old campaigner

But there was life in the middle-aged dog yet. In 1806, at the age of forty-three, and eleven years since his last actual fight, Daniel took on a much younger boxer, Harry Lee, and beat him over fifty-three rounds. Even more remarkable, on July 4, 1820, at the age of fifty-seven, he fought twelve rounds with Tom Owens (a former title claimant and incidentally inventor of the dumb-bell) on Banstead Downs. Admittedly Owens was himself fifty-two and Mendoza lost, but he must have had the constitution of a horse. He survived another sixteen years, dying in 1836, aged seventy-three.

Royal bodyguard

Although John Jackson retired after taking the title from Mendoza – and it was only his third major fight – he was regarded as champion for some five or six years. His gymnasium in Bond Street, patronised by the nobility – one of his pupils was Lord Byron, who dubbed him 'Emperor of Pugilism' – was the headquarters of the sport for the first quarter of the 19th century. His poshest patron was the Prince Regent, who, at his coronation as George IV, in 1821, had eighteen prominent pugilists dressed as pages, to guard the approaches to Westminster Hall!

Bristol fashion

But the prize-ring character who really made it in respectable society was the remarkable John Gully – the champion who fought only two men professionally and lost to one of them! His was a real rags to riches story. After Jackson's retirement the heavyweight crown eventually passed to Jem Belcher, a butcher from Bristol (the nursery of so many famous pugilists) and a grandson of Jack Slack. But in 1803, when only twenty-two, Jem lost an eye while playing racquets. Despite this handicap, two years later he disputed fellow Bristolian Henry Pearce's claim to the title but was beaten in eighteen rounds.

Gully, yet another Bristolian, was languishing in Kings Bench Prison for debt when he was visited by the new champ, nicknamed 'The Game Chicken' from the abbreviation of his first name, Hen. Gully, a keen amateur boxer, put on the mufflers and sparred with Pearce to such good effect that the champion persuaded a wealthy member of the Fancy to pay Gully's debts on condition that he contend for the title.

That match took place at Hailsham, Sussex, on October 8, 1805, and was watched by the Duke of Clarence, the future King William IV. The contestants' friendship outside the ring was apparently forgotten, for they hammered away at each other for an hour and seventeen minutes when, after the sixty-fourth round, Gully gave Pearce best.

It was only two months after that gruelling bout that Pearce confirmed his superiority over Belcher. But, stricken with consumption, Pearce did not fight again and in 1809 died, aged thirty-two.

Giant killer

On his retirement, 'The Game Chicken' passed his title to

Gully as the only man fit to succeed him. But only after Gully had stopped his chief rival, Bob Gregson, the Lancashire Giant, in thirty-six rounds on February 14, 1807, at Newmarket, was he acknowledged undisputed champ.

Gregson again challenged and this time, on May 10, 1808, Gully won in twenty-eight rounds. The champion then announced to the crowd that he would never fight again.

Derby winner . . .

And he never did. Instead, he took a London pub, became a bookmaker, winning a fortune on both horses and boxers. He then took to horse breeding, with considerable success. His Margrave won the 1832 St Leger. In 1846, he won both the Derby, with Pyrrhus the First, and the 1,000 Guineas, with Mendicant. In 1854 he again won the Derby, with Andover, and the 2,000 Guineas, with The Hermit.

. . . and M.P.

In 1832, possibly for a bet, he stood as Liberal candidate for Pontefract and was elected, serving for five years. He put much of his winnings into property, owning several collieries and an estate, Ackworth Park, in Durham, where he died in 1863, aged seventy-nine. And as if that were not enough, he had twenty-four children, by two wives!

First knight

It is said that John Gully could also have been the first boxer to be knighted, but he declined the accolade. So that distinction went instead, according to popular belief at least, to Ireland's first real champion, Daniel Donnelly. His greatest fight was against George Cooper, an Englishman, whom he defeated in eleven storming rounds at the Curragh of Kildare on December 13, 1815.

The Lord Lieutenant of Ireland gave a banquet in the champion's honour and, at George IV's behest, dubbed him Sir Daniel. So the story goes, though there is no documentary proof of its truth. 'Sir' Dan later gave exhibition tours in England and Ireland, but he was as fond of wine and women as he was of fighting and he died in 1820, aged thirty-two.

An old soldier told us that when he was stationed at Curragh Camp in 1914 he often visited Donnelly's Hollow where the famous fight with Cooper took place. The Hollow was about fifty yards across and some thirty feet deep and leading into it from each side were deep footprints which met in the middle where the two men fought toe to toe. According to other readers, those footprints were still to be seen in the mid-1960s. Possibly they still are, preserved by the little folk, no doubt.

Black v. white

We Old Pair once got away with a technical low blow when we agreed with a reader that the first recorded bout between a white man and a coloured man was that between Tom Cribb and Tom Molineaux in 1810. Normally such a gaffe on our part would be instantly spotted by hawk-eyed readers who would clamour for a published correction, but for some reason that one passed unnoticed. Now we are pleased to acknowledge the foul and put the record straight.

In fact there is an account of an unknown negro beating one Treadwell in Marylebone in 1791, but the first to make his name in Britain was Bill Richmond, born on Staten Island, New York, in 1763, and brought to England in his teens by General Earl Percy, later Duke of Northumberland.

After several victories and only one defeat in the prize-ring, on October 8, 1805, at Hailsham, he challenged the up and coming Tom Cribb, the man who three years later was to take over Gully's championship. The negro was giving away 1½st and eighteen years to the Englishman, but he fought gamely for an hour and a half before being knocked out. Nevertheless, Richmond went on to chalk up some ten victories, including one at the age of fifty-five.

Meanwhile, he also was teaching the noble art and had taken under his wing another negro, Tom Molineaux, who came over in 1809 and convincingly defeated two of Cribb's proteges in short order.

Cribb, having beaten Gregson and Belcher, had more or less retired as undefeated champion, but when the American claimed the British title he had no option but to accept the challenge. This fact made the Cribb v. Molineaux contest the first to arouse not only the interest of the Fancy but of the whole British public.

Dirty tricks department

It took place on Copthorne Common, near East Grinstead, Sussex, on a bitterly cold December 18, 1810, the weather putting the man from Virginia at a disadvantage from the start. Apart from that, the pair were physically well matched. For the first few rounds it was anybody's fight, but gradually the American began to wear his opponent down until, after twenty-eight rounds, it seemed Cribb would be unable to continue. There then occurred one of those incidents which have happened more than once since in other big sports events when not only personal fortunes but national prestige has been at stake. With Cribb near collapse, one of his seconds, Joe Ward – the other was the famed Gully – accused Bill Richmond, Molineaux's second, of putting lead weights in the challenger's fists. This was a flagrant lie, but the ensuing uproar gave Cribb time to recover and after another five rounds the negro fell, exhausted from his exertions and the cold, and retired.

After his narrow escape, it seems Cribb was reluctant to give Molineaux a return, but the negro again forced the champion's hand by offering to fight any man in the land. This challenge was accepted by one Joe Rimmer. Beating him over twenty-one rounds on May 21, 1811, Molineaux again claimed the title, thus compelling Cribb to uphold England's honour once more.

Fit to bust

And this time Cribb made no mistake. The fight was arranged for September 28, 1811, at Thistleton Gap, near Wymondham, Leicestershire. Nine weeks before the event Cribb's patron, Captain Barclay, a physical fitness expert who had once walked a thousand miles in as many hours for a bet, took Cribb up to the Scottish Highlands for rigorous training by which he reduced the champion's flabby 16st to under 13½st.

The effect was dramatic. A crowd of 20,000-plus saw Cribb hammer Molineaux to defeat in only nineteen minutes, smashing the negro's jaw in the eleventh round.

The champion made a triumphal tour back to London but he never fought again. Instead, he sponsored the next champion, Tom Spring, whom he later adopted as his son.

Cribb died in Woolwich in his sixty-eighth year. Poor Molineaux continued fighting for several years but took to drink and died in an army barracks in Ireland while touring with a boxing show, on August 4, 1818. He was thirty-four.

Classic punch-up

The arrival of Tom Spring in the ring brings us back to where we came in on this chapter, Hazlitt's essay *The Fight.* For the bout he described was virtually what would now be termed an 'eliminator' for a crack at the title which Cribb had bestowed upon his protege, Spring. Hazlitt's account has become a classic, not merely for his report on the fight itself but for the manner in which he captured the whole atmosphere of the proceedings, the journey to the venue by stagecoach, the characters of the Fancy he met, including Cribb and Gully and one or two whose names he discreetly disguises, in particular 'Tom Turtle', a trainer.

This last character has been identified as John Thurtle, a Norwich man who arranged many fights and taught the rudiments of the art to George Borrow, author of *Lavengro.* In 1824 he was hanged at Hertford for the murder of a gambling associate and it is said that his last wish was to read Pierce Egan's account of the title fight between Spring and Jack Langan which had just taken place!

Gasman was no gent

But back to Hazlitt. Probably the charm of his essay is that he writes with the eagerness and freshness of a man seeing his first fight and he makes no bones about his own partiality. Apparently Tom Hickman, the Gasman, so named for his flashy brilliance, was a whirlwind fighter who had scored several quick knockouts. But he was also a braggart and a bully and Hazlitt would have none of that: 'It was not manly, 'twas not fighter-like . . . Modesty should accompany the Fancy as its shadow.'

But the writer's indignation is nicely tempered with humour: 'A boxer was bound to beat his man, but not to thrust his fist, either actually or by implication, in every one's face. Even a highwayman, in the way of trade, may blow out your brains, but if he uses foul language at the same time, I should say he was no gentleman.'

And for all that it was his first fight, the essayist seemed to know instinctively what has since become a maxim of the fight game, that a good big 'un will always beat a good little 'un. For he observes: 'The difference of weight between the two combatants (14 stone to 12) was nothing to the sporting men. Great, heavy, clumsy, long-armed Bill Neate kicked the beam in the scale of the Gas-man's vanity. The amateurs were frightened at his big words, and thought that they would make up for the difference of six feet and five feet nine. Truly, the Fancy are not men of imagination. They judge of what has been, and cannot conceive of anything that is to be. The Gas-man had won hitherto; therefore he must beat a man half as big as himself . . .'

Gory details

Hazlitt dedicated his essay to the ladies: 'nor let it seem out of character for the fair to notice the exploits of the brave . . . listen with a subdued air and without shuddering, to a tale tragic only in appearance . . .' But if his fair readers got that far, we imagine they reached for the smelling salts when they read this description of Hickman after one knockdown: 'His face was like a human skull, a death's head, spouting blood. The eyes were filled with blood, the nose streamed with blood, the mouth gaped blood.'

But we must resist giving you the complete account of the fight. Suffice it to say that Bill Neate won in the eighteenth round. That victory, helped in no small measure by the publicity given it when Hazlitt's account was published in the *New Monthly Magazine* of February, 1822, earned him a title fight with Spring.

They met at Hinckley Downs on May 17, 1823, and, alas for the Bristol Bull, the new champion proved worthy of Cribb's mantle. Neate had to give in after thirty-seven minutes, having fought the last two of the eight rounds with a broken arm.

Fighting words

The Hickman-Neate fight was immortalised by the genius of a first class writer, but there were many lesser fistic affairs which made good copy for contemporary newspaper reporters. Possibly their style was less 'literary' than Hazlitt's but it set the pattern for colourful sports reporting still to be found in the popular Press.

The following account of a prize-fight which took place on Barlow Fell, Co. Durham, on October 25, 1824, was sent to us by reader James Pell, of Gosforth, Newcastle. We enjoyed it so much that we re-published it, practically verbatim, in the Live Letters column over four consecutive days. The pugilists were Tom Dunn, butcher, and Jem Wallace, bricklayer, and they fought for a purse of forty sovereigns. Unfortunately the reporter was anonymous, but he was certainly well versed in the vernacular of the Fancy:

'On arriving at the ground, we were somewhat disappointed at finding so few carriages: the rough commoners, yokels and men of metal, mustered strong, and a few Corinthian swells appeared on their prads. Three or four heavy drags and tumblers with a few rumblers, afforded the principal stands.

'Much time was lost in making a ring, and the rain fell for about a quarter of an hour. It cleared up, and at ten minutes after one, Wallace shewed, but the ring, by the rush, was instantly broke and the ropes and stakes were trod underfoot. Wallace was taken back to the coach and so much difficulty was experienced in forming a ring, that it was even betting there would be no fight.

'However after some delay, the inner one was again formed, and by dint of beating out, and two horsemen riding round the outside, an outer one was formed, both of which were pretty well kept by the horsemen riding round betwixt them the whole of the fight.

'The men entered the ring with their seconds: Frank Blackett picked up Dunn, and J. Hutchinson waited upon Wallace. On peeling, the difference between them was great. Tom looked the heaviest, but his flesh was loose and fat. He seemed to be all the worse for the training, while Wallace had the advantage in height, length of arm and was in tip-top condition. Both seemed confident, and a prime mill was anticipated. At twenty-three minutes before two commenced:

Round one

'The lads had scarce shook hands and thrown themselves

into their attitudes (which were beautiful) before they commenced, each eager to administer. Wallace received a teaser on the left cheek, which tinged the looker a trifle and changed the colour of the flesh so that many thought it was "first blood". This round was decided in favour of Dunn, though he seemed rather blown.

Second round
'Wallace put in his fives so rapidly that both Dunn's ogles were taken measure of for a suit of mourning, and the blood was flowing so freely from his upperworks that it seemed he had mounted the Guards' uniform – red with blue facings. Tom floored by a tremendous blow.

Third round
'Tom received a snorter on the smeller, which brought the claret in streams: a sharp rally which ended by Wallace grassing his man with terrible effect. It was "bellows to mend" with Tom, who shewed symptoms of great weakness. 2 to 1 on Wallace.

Round four
'Being brought up to the "scratch" again, it was evident Tom was nearly done up; one peeper had taken its departure, and the other was fast going the same road. Wallace appeared with increased confidence, and planted such a right-handed hit on Tom's jugular that he went down quite groggy.

Fifth round
'Wallace now went to work and let fly right and left on Tom's face and neck; and it was ditto, ditto, ditto, to the end of the chapter. Tom's second busy with the brandy bottle.

Sixth round
'Tom could not stand the punishing blows of his opponent – there was too much Cayenne in the seasoning to be at all palatable. He then made a weak attempt to rally, when he was grassed by an astonisher. Any odds on Wallace.

Seventh round
'Tom appeared at the scratch with alacrity on the call of

"Time", and appeared as if he had got second wind. Hit for hit was the order of the day. Tom put in a nice one upon Wallace's ribs, but tasted a queer one in return upon his nob. A manly struggle ensued for the throw, when Tom went down and Wallace fell heavily upon him. The restorative was again applied, but the throw semed to have taken the last puff of wind out of his body.

Eighth round

'Tom came up once more, but was chopt by a most tremendous right-handed hit in the head. It was evident that he had not a chance, and the contest was resigned.

'Lots of blunt changed owners on this occasion, as, indeed, might easily be discovered by the many long faces among the homeward-bound, which plainly announced – Pockets To Let.'

Stirring stuff, indeed. After reading that little lot we felt like getting busy with the brandy bottle ourselves!

One for the scrapbook

We must go forward some fourteen years to meet the next of the prize-fighters featured in Live Letters. The champions, as we have seen, often enjoyed the type of hero-worship now reserved mostly for Soccer stars, and to have entered the ring with one of the 'greats' was something to be recorded in a family history.

Dennis Millington, of Fenwick, Doncaster, S. Yorks, wrote to us about just such a brief brush with fame in his family's past:

'My dear late wife's maternal grandfather, Jake Bradbury of Annerley Woodhouse, Notts, was a noted character for growing roses – and for fighting. He would rather fight than do anything else and he would take on anyone. He was reputed to have fought one "Bendigo" in Newark market place and I'm wondering if you can tell me who this "Bendigo" was.

We could indeed, for, though perhaps not the greatest of champions, Bold Bendigo was probably the most colourful. Born in Nottingham in 1811, his real name was William Thompson. He was one of triplets, inevitably, in a church-going family, nicknamed Shadrach, Meshach and Abednego. Incidentally, he was the last of his mother's twenty-one children!

He started prize-fighting in 1832 and in the next five years chalked up some sixteen wins, most of them in short, sharp bouts. In 1835, however, he had fought Ben Caunt, four years his junior and known as Big Ben for his 6ft 2ins height and 14½st. Bendigo weighed only 11½st and was five inches shorter. The experienced Bendigo relied on his speed, hitting and running, ducking and weaving. It was Caunt's first real fight against a pro and he became infuriated by his tactics. At the end of the twenty-second round he rushed across the ring, and shouted at Bendigo to fight like a man. Bendigo's reply isn't recorded, but it provoked Caunt to hit him while he was still sitting and Caunt was disqualified.

Fall guy

Thus the two became bitter rivals. They met twice more, and on both occasions the result was far from satisfactory.

On April 3, 1838, at Selby, Yorks, they battled for seventy-four rounds and Caunt was taking terrific punishment when, in the seventy-fifth Bendigo slipped and fell. Caunt's seconds immediately called for Bendigo's disqualification, falling without being hit being a foul under the rules. The referee upheld their claim. At that, Bendigo's supporters rioted and Caunt was lucky to escape them.

Caunt now claimed the championship but in the meantime a former champion, James 'Deaf' Burke, had returned to England from America, maintaining that he was still champion and willing to meet any challenger.

Five years earlier at St Albans, Herts, Deaf Burke had won the longest championship fight on record – ninety-nine rounds lasting three hours and sixteen minutes – against the Irish champion, Simon Byrne, who was so badly beaten that he died three days later.

The Deaf 'Un then went to America where on May 6, 1836, in New Orleans, he fought another Irishman, Sam O'Rourke, who said he wanted to avenge Byrne's death. After three rounds, when Burke was well on top, O'Rourke's supporters broke the ring and Burke had to run for his life.

Back in England, Burke's renewed claim to the championship was denied by Bendigo, who stopped him in ten rounds at Heather, Leicestershire, on February 12, 1839.

Third encounter

Having injured his left kneecap, Bendigo went into retirement for five years but then his old adversary Ben Caunt, who had also been to America, turned up again and claimed the title, making their third match inevitable. It took place at Stoney Stratford on September 9, 1845, and was even more gruelling than their previous bouts. It went on for ninety-three rounds, during which Caunt more than once tried to break Bendigo's back across the ropes. But the old warrior's punches told and in the ninety-third the exhausted Caunt fell without being hit and was disqualified.

Bendigo fought only once more, five years later, at the age of thirty-nine, and again won on a foul when his opponent, Tom Paddock, hit him while he was down.

We could find no record of him fighting reader Millington's wife's grandfather, Jake Bradbury, but then records of those old-timers were often incomplete because the sport was illegal and the participants were frequently jailed for breaking the peace.

From prison to pulpit

Indeed, Bendigo was allegedly imprisoned no less than twenty-eight times – once being 'shopped' by one of his own brothers. On the last occasion, he was converted by the prison chaplain and became a Nonconformist minister and popular preacher at revivalist meetings.

Reader E. Syson, of Beeston, Notts, told us a nice story in that connection:

'At one of Bendigo's meetings, after patiently withstanding a drunken heckler, he eventually said: "Excuse me, Lord", stepped down from the rostrum, dealt smartly with the nuisance, then resumed preaching as though nothing had happened. I hope this story is true.'

Well, if it isn't, it should be. And we can well believe it, for Bendigo was a natural clown and was fond of making up poems about his exploits which he sent to various newspapers – does that ring a bell somehow? Other readers sent us a monologue on Bendigo's life, allegedly composed by Sir Arthur Conan Doyle.

Another Bendigo admirer, Miss Margaret Fletcher, of Nottingham, told us how her father used to take her walking on summer Sundays to a circle of trees known as Bendigo's Ring, where the champ used to train. Miss Fletcher is also in correspondence with the Bendigo Club, in the town of Bendigo, in Victoria, Australia. And if that isn't evidence enough of his fame, there is even a beer named after him!

Bendigo died in his sixty-ninth year, on August 23, 1880, after falling downstairs in his home at Beeston. Eleven years later, Nottingham erected a monument in the form of a sleeping lion to its bravest son. The inscription reads: 'In life always brave, fighting like a lion; in death like a lamb, tranquil in Zion.'

The greatest?

Relics and trophies of the great pugilists turn up in unexpected places and sometimes they have been reported to us by readers quite unaware of their significance. For example, Mr T. Steel, of Knaresborough, Yorks, wrote to ask us about a clay pipe he had dug up. On the bowl were the likenesses of two boxers in the classic pose of barefist fighters. Above one was the legend 'Tom Sayers', above the other 'J. C. Hee . . .', the rest of the name being indecipherable.

Similarly, S. Gadsden, of Grays, Essex, wrote:

'We have a beautiful silver mug which bears the inscription: "Presented to TOM SAYERS, Champion of England, for his Brave and Manly Conduct in and out of the Ring, by Cha. Good, Lamb & Flag, Bristol, Aug. 16, 1860". Can you tell me anything about Tom Sayers?'

We imagine the Gadsdens polished their silver mug with even more care, perhaps even some reverence, after we related Sayer's history, for he is rated by many of his contemporaries, and by modern students of pugilism, as the finest of all who stepped into the prize-ring.

And the name that Mr Steel couldn't quite make out on his pipe was J. C. (John Carmel) Heenan, the American heavyweight champion, and Tom's opponent in the most famous barefist battle in history.

Blind pluck

Born in Pimlico, Brighton, on May 25, 1826, the son of a cobbler, Sayers was, in fact, really only a middleweight, weighing no more than 10st 12lb at his heaviest, and standing only 5ft 8½ins. Yet such was his skill and stamina – developed by his early trade as a bricklayer – that he took on most of the heavyweights of his day and was beaten only once. That was on October 18, 1853, against Nat Langham, a stone heavier than Tom and himself a skilled boxer. Langham concentrated on the smaller man's eyes and by the fifty-ninth round had closed them both. Sayers fought on, blind, for two more rounds before his seconds refused to allow him to continue.

And on January 29, 1856, the Sayers v. Harry Poulson fight lasted 109 rounds over 3 hours 8 minutes – only eight minutes shorter than the record Burke v. Byrne contest – before Poulson was beaten.

Sayers won the heavyweight championship from William Perry, the Tipton Slasher, on June 16, 1857. The Slasher, a six-footer and more than 2½st heavier, dwarfed Sayers, who nevertheless thrashed the giant in ten rounds.

Four more victories – including one over Tom Paddock, Bendigo's last opponent – confirmed Sayer's right to the title before he accepted the challenge from Heenan, famed in the United States as 'The Benicia Boy'.

Fight of the century

The match created even more patriotic fervour than the Cribb v. Molineaux affair fifty years earlier. Both men were acknowledged champions of their country and communications had greatly improved so that what was properly the first world heavyweight championship was covered by British and American newspapers. It was attended by a huge crowd from all walks of life, including celebrities such as Thackeray and Dickens, and a number of MPs. One commentator observed that 'Parliament had been emptied to patronise a prize-fight.' Some fans even came over from the Continent.

Yet the affair was, strictly speaking, illegal. While training, Heenan complained that he 'had been chased out of eight counties'. Sayers finished his training at Newmarket and travelled to London secretly in a horsebox.

The two met for the first time at dawn on the day of the fight, April 17, 1860, both disguised, at London Bridge station from which two special trains, packed with spectators, were to leave for a supposedly 'unknown' destination. Obviously the Metropolitan Police could have stopped the whole thing there and then, but they merely watched the track for fifteen miles to make sure the fight did not take place within the Metropolitan boundary.

David and Goliath

The venue was, in fact, Farnborough, Hants. When the contestants stripped off, some British hearts must have been daunted, for the American was huge, 6ft 2ins and a pound short of 14st – 6ins taller and nearly 3½st heavier than their hero. But Sayers had played David to more than one Goliath and his accurate punches drew first blood. By sheer weight, however, Heenan threw the Englishman to the ground again and again. He was also a tremendous hitter and early on ruptured a tendon in Sayers's right arm – some say the arm was actually broken.

Now the experience of his one defeat at the hands of Langan stood Sayers in good stead, for he proceeded to close Heenan's eyes so that by the thirty-fourth round he was virtually blind. Furthermore, the American apparently had neglected to harden his hands – pugilists steeped them in brine – and they swelled so much it appeared he was wearing boxing gloves.

Then, in the thirty-seventh round, Heenan rushed Sayers to the ropes and seemed about to throttle him. The crowd went wild and cut the ropes, the police intervened and the referee left the ring. Nevertheless, the fight continued for another five rounds until, after two hours twenty minutes, it was finally abandoned.

Both men claimed the victory, but it was officially judged a draw and both were awarded a championship belt. The American Press stated that their champion had been beaten by the British mob, but to Heenan's great credit he absolved Sayers from blame. The two champions later went on tour together and when, three years later, the Benicia Boy returned to England to fight the new English champion, Tom King, Sayers acted as his second.

But the great fight at Farnborough had really been too much for both participants. Heenan was now no match for

King, who beat him comfortably in thirty-five minutes. That was the Benicia Boy's last fight. He died, aged thirty-eight, in Wyoming.

Sayers never recovered his health. Little more than five years after Farnborough, on November 7, 1865, he died, probably from TB and diabetes, though there was a story that he had been poisoned. He was thirty-nine.

End of an era

But let us end this parade of the pugilists on a more cheerful note. In February, 1975, we published a letter from Bill Hadfield, of Prince George, British Columbia, who wanted us to settle a wager over the birthplace of Jem Mace, last of the bareknuckle champions of England. Was it Beeston, Notts, or Beeston, Yorks, asked Bill?

It was neither. Beeston, Notts, was the home of Bendigo, but Jem 'The Gipsy' Mace was born at Beeston-next-Mileham, near King's Lynn, Norfolk, on April 8, 1831. He had a long and dignified career as a prize-fighter but unfortunately for him was at his prime when, following the outcry at the brutality and rioting in the Sayers v. Heenan contest, the authorities made a determined effort to clamp down on the sport. His third fight with Joe Goss, on August 6, 1866, which he won in twenty-one rounds, was really the last barefist championship bout in England, although the sport continued, on a lesser level, into the 1890s. Mace later fought in Australia and America, then returned to England where he gave exhibitions under the more acceptable Queensberry Rules and wearing gloves, into his sixties. He remained active until his death at seventy-nine.

Gipsy's blessing

There was a happy sequel to our reply to Bill Hadfield. Five months later we heard from him again:

'Among many letters I received after you published my question about Jem Mace was a well-written note from a Master Kenneth Parke, simply bursting with pride that The Gipsy was a son of the village where he attends school. We correspond and it seems I have sparked a keen interest in Kenneth and his fellow pupils' natural history and geography lessons with my descriptions of Canada and the wildlife there. Now I am rounding up my fellow Limeys to put the bite on them on behalf of the Beeston-next-Mileham Church Tower Fund. Not only Prince George is involved – Ottawa and Edmonton are also being softened up under the Old Pals Act. We can't help the old country much in her present difficulties, but at least we can help preserve the church tower in one of her pleasant villages.'

We ancient arbiters were delighted at such an outcome – and we reckon old Jem Mace would have been knocked out by it, too!

POSTMAN'S KNOCK

CONSIDERING that letters are our life's blood, so to speak – we receive about a thousand of them every week – and that this is the fourth volume of our Little Black Book, we think it high time that we included something about that remarkable institution, the Post Office.

We use the adjective 'remarkable' advisedly, for it is just that. With more than 400,000 employees, it is the biggest employer of labour in Britain. It provides a range of services probably unequalled by any other organisation in the world. And not the least of its functions is that of keeping us Old Pair in a job!

We can't possibly attempt to give a history of the Post Office here, merely some of the more important facts and figures and odder aspects of the service which have featured in our mailbag. But first we might as well correct the commonly held suspicion that the whole thing started with the introduction of the famous Penny Black Stamp in 1840.

Private letters were being carried by post horses at least as early as 1548, in which year a statute fixed the rate at a penny a mile, and the office of 'Chief Postmaster' of England seems to have existed in Henry VIII's time.

In 1657, an Act was passed establishing the office of Postmaster-General of England and giving him control of all persons 'riding in posts'. No other person was to be permitted to 'set up or employ any foot posts, horse posts or pacquet boats'. And in 1660, the year Charles II returned to England, the General Letter Office was founded.

Royal mail order

Despite this, in 1680 a chap named William Dockwra established his own Penny Post for the London area. For one penny Dockwra would carry, registered and insured, letters and parcels up to a pound in weight and £10 in value. He set up seven sorting and district offices, and more than 400 receiving houses and wall-boxes.

There were hourly collections, with ten deliveries daily in central London and six in the suburbs. Places such as Hackney and Islington, which were then outlying villages, had four deliveries.

But Dockwra's enterprise landed him in hot water. King Charles II had already approved 'an Act for settling the Profits of the Post Office on the Duke of York, and his Heirs-Male.' And the Duke, peeved at his perks being poached, sued Dockwra for infringement of his patent and the penny post became part of the general post.

Dockwra later received a pension of £500 a year in compensation.

Country walks

Mr E. Nicholls, of Worcester, once sent us the following excerpts from an account of a penny post, found in Sir Samuel Morland's Perpetual Almanack, dated 1739: '. . . and considering divers of these places are remote, it is desired you put in your letters and parcels before six of the clock overnight at the Receiving Houses from whence they will be collected and brought into their proper offices, because divers of the country messengers go on their walks by six of the clock next morning and thereby will gain a day's time in the delivery, but for those places that are nearer letters are collected and delivered two or three times a day.'

Sir Samuel's list of Receiving Houses included some quaint names – Black Mary's Hole, Cold Bath, Boarded River and Holloway Up and Down.

Up hill!

But it was Rowland Hill, a Wiltshire man interested in mathematics and mechanical inventions, who literally put the stamp on the Post Office as we know it. In 1837 he wrote a pamphlet, *Post Office Reform; its Importance and Practicability*, in which he advocated a uniform penny postage throughout Britain. At that time the postal rate depended on the weight and contents of a letter and the distance carried. A letter between two London addresses cost 2d, but if carried for twenty miles the fee was 6d. And at that rate the letter was restricted to only one sheet. For two sheets the rate was doubled and a letter weighing 2oz cost seven times the minimum.

Hill argued that these rates grossly exceeded the actual cost, which he estimated to be rather less than one-tenth of a penny for a single letter. Acknowledging that the fraction would be impossible to collect, he suggested the all-in penny rate as the only practical alternative.

The proposal was ridiculed by vested interests and Post Office officials who said the loss in revenue would be ruinous. However public demand led to a committee of inquiry which resulted in the Act of 1839 establishing a uniform rate of 1d per half ounce or 2d per ounce, any fraction of an ounce over the first being reckoned as an ounce.

Black and blue queen

Thus the world's first adhesive postage stamps, which went on sale on May 6, 1840, were the 1d black and 2d blue. The design of the stamps had been the subject of a public competition, for which four prizes were awarded. But the chosen design was the joint effort of Hill himself, Charles and Frederick Heath, William Wyon and Henry Corbould, the profile of Queen Victoria having already been used on Wyon's medal struck to commemorate Victoria's accession in 1837.

In the event, the famous penny black was issued for only a few months. In 1841 the colour was changed to red and the 2d blue had white lines added above and below the head and the printing ink was changed. This was done to prevent the stamp being used a second time – the original black made it difficult to see if the stamp had been postmarked and with the original blue ink the postmark could be rubbed out.

Mail chauvinists

Readers often ask why it is that every country except Britain has its name on its postage stamps. The reason is that, as described above, we invented 'em so, by international agreement, ours are the only stamps which don't have to state the country of origin. And quite right, too!

Incidentally, up to 1854, when Henry Archer invented the perforating machine, stamps were issued in block sheets from which they had to be cut out as required.

First class row

The basic rate for inland letters remained at one penny from 1840 until 1918, when it was raised to 1½d. In 1920 it went up to 2d, was lowered to 1½d in 1922, staying at that rate until 1940, when it became 2½d. Up to 3d in 1951, it remained thus until 1965, when it was increased by another 1d.

Then on September 16, 1968, the controversial two-tier system was introduced. Initially the first class rate was 5d, second class 4d, the idea being that second class mail would normally be delivered up to two working days later than the first class. In practice, at least according to many readers who complained to us, there often appeared to be no difference in the speed of delivery no matter what rate of postage was paid.

Also the subject of some doubt was whether an envelope bearing two stamps totalling the first class rate would be passed by automatic sorting machines as first class mail – or did it have to be just one stamp to the value of the first class rate?

Frank answer

The Post Office assured us that it doesn't matter how many stamps are put on a letter to go first class, provided the value adds up to the first class rate. Much of this sorting is now done electronically by a machine called an Automatic Letter Franker in which ultra violet rays 'count' the phosphor bars in the stamps.

Bags of mail

But back to Rowland Hill. Official prejudice against his scheme was proved groundless by the following statistics. In the week immediately preceding the introduction of the uniform penny rate the number of letters delivered in the United Kingdom totalled 1,585,973. Within ten years the weekly total rose to nearly 7,000,000 and within twenty years the Post Office's net annual revenue was back to its 1838 figure – £1,652,424 – and this after several large pensions had been paid off.

That, of course, is very small beer by today's standards. In 1977-78 the Post Office's income was £4,183 million, of which £367,700,000 was profit. Most of that profit came from the telecommunications side, but the postal business alone showed a surplus of £40,400,000. And in that year the Post Office transmitted 160 million parcels and 9,325 million other pieces of mail, including 8,840 million inland letters. It provides a daily delivery service to 22 million addresses.

The magnitude of the task of handling such a volume of

mail is even more staggering when you consider that there are only some 1,600 post offices in Britain run directly by the Post Office, supported by 21,300 sub-post offices, usually run as agencies in conjunction with private businesses.

Paper weights

Talking of staggering, we are often asked what weight a postman is required to carry in his delivery bag. It's a hefty 34lb for postmen on foot, 49½lb on bikes, and 70lb on those tricycle trolleys.

It's curious how many of our older readers remember the cone-shaped peaked helmets postmen used to wear, and ask us to supply the name for them. They were called 'shakos' and were replaced by peaked caps in 1932.

Another regular question is: are postmen allowed to do the football pools? The official reply we got to that was: 'Officers of the Post Office may participate in ordinary football pools, but they must not gamble'. If doing the pools isn't a gamble, we wonder why our lad George is forever asking us for advances in his wages!

Hard luck, mate!

But perhaps that concession to its officers is by way of an acknowledgment to Messrs Vernons, Littlewoods et al. for the vast amount of business they bring to the Post Office, not only in postage but in postal orders.

A pools punter whose coupon and postal order were returned to him, having been misdelivered, asked if the Post Office would have made good his loss if the coupon forecast had been correct. The official answer to that is that the Post Office is not legally bound to pay anything 'for injury or damage consequent on the loss, damage, delay, non-delivery or mis-delivery' of anything sent by unregistered letter.

Funny money

The first postal orders, by the bye, were issued on January 1, 1881. Mr T. Sheldon, of Hanging Heaton, Yorks, remembered using postal orders as ordinary money at the start of the Second World War, but friends of his own age thought he was mistaken. Nevertheless he was right. Postal orders were used as legal tender from the day war was declared, September 3, 1939, until December 20, 1939. This was because of a heavy run on ordinary currency. A similar thing happened at the start of the First World War, when postal orders were used as currency from August 7, 1914, until February 4, 1915.

Mystery machine

One postal order poser we weren't able to solve entirely to our satisfaction was put to us by Mr N. Young, of London SE25:

'About 1949 or 1950, I bought some postal orders from a machine in Birmingham Post Office. The machine was rather like an adding machine, with figures on the top and a handle at the side.

'Now my friends at work say there have never been machines to issue postal orders, but I'm sure I'm right.'

The problem was that the date of Mr Young's memory didn't tie in with the facts as far as we could ascertain them. Some sixty machines for dispensing two bob and half-crown postal orders were put into various post offices throughout the country – but that was in the early 1960s. Anyway, they were an experimental idea which didn't seem to catch on. We can't think why, though, for they would surely have saved time in counter queues.

Novelist's idea

One of the earliest of the postal time-savers, one that we all take for granted, is the pillar box, for which boon we are indebted to Victorian author Anthony Trollope. As well as writing numerous novels – *Barchester Towers* and the Palliser saga being the best-known – and several books on travel, Trollope was for many years a Post Office official. He started as a clerk in 1834, but in 1841, having got into difficulties over debts and women, went to Ireland as a surveyor. Returning to England, he was appointed inspector of rural deliveries and for two years toured Britain on horseback. As a result of his observations he recommended collecting boxes in remote districts as an alternative to more expensive Post Offices. The first was erected in Jersey, in the Channel Islands, in November, 1852. It was constructed by a local blacksmith who made a gaffe by putting on the Royal

Arms of the old King, William IV, instead of those of Victoria!

Antique collector

The second, which is still in use, is at St Peter Port, Guernsey, erected in February, 1853, in which year they were introduced to the mainland. The oldest 1853 pillar boxes in England are still in use at Bishop's Caundle, Dorset, and Framlingham, Suffolk.

Incidentally, Trollope finally left the Post Office in 1866, when he failed to be given the expected appointment of an assistant secretaryship. But his pillar boxes weren't our familiar friends dressed in red with black caps – up to 1874 they were all painted green. One of the original Channel Islands boxes, still in its original green, can be seen outside South Western Postal Region Headquarters at Old Market, Bristol, where it was transplanted to commemorate the independence of Guernsey Post Office, in 1969, when the British Post Office became a public corporation.

Air mail blue

You won't be old enough to remember those, but do you remember blue letter boxes? They were introduced, for 'air mail only' in London in May, 1930, and later throughout the country. Blue-liveried vans were also used for air mail collections until August, 1938, by which time most overseas mail was airborne anyway. The first official air mail was carried between Hendon and Windsor as early as 1911, by Gustav Hamel, the original intrepid aviator.

But we digress. In 1856 pillar boxes in the form of fluted Doric columns appeared, some with vertical apertures, some with horizontal. Some eleven examples of these can still be found throughout the country. And there are eight specimens of the first national standard pillar box, introduced in 1859, still in use, five of them in Liverpool.

Any old iron?

Age lends value, as well as charm, to many objects of the Victorian era. The 'classic' Victorian pillar box was the hexagonal shape with 'acorn' top designed by J. Penfold, which model was standard from 1866-1879, seventy-six of which are still in service. In 1966 the Post Office would sell obsolete Penfolds for their scrap value of £4 each.

As the craze for collecting Victoriana grew, waiting lists of applicants for old pillar boxes were drawn up – and the price rose accordingly. By 1976 the Post Office were inviting 'offers in excess of £500' for a Penfold, and two years later the asking price was around £700!

That inflationary trend will no doubt be of interest to the Marquess of Bath, who once wrote to us:

'I own a cast-off Edward VIII pillar box – I collect anything appertaining to that gentleman. Can you tell me how many of his pillar boxes are still in use, and whether any Edward VIII wall boxes exist?'

Rare find

At that time, 1967, we were led to believe there were 120 pillar boxes bearing the insignia of the abdicated king. However, we have since learned from the Letter Box Study Group – who kindly supplied us with much of our information on this section – that there are 135 Edward VIII letter boxes, the Group's members having conducted a nation-wide search. We also told the Marquess, on good authority, that he had no chance of adding an Edward VIII wall box to his collection, for only half a dozen were made and after his abdication they were all fitted with George VI doors. But again the LBS Group's sleuths tracked down one which had slipped through the net and still has its original door, Bawdsey, Suffolk, Post Office.

Suffolk has another collector's item, a wall box of 1859 vintage. There are five examples of the first (1857) wall boxes, sited away from Post Offices, but the only survivor of the 1859 design can be seen at Boyden End, Wickhambrook, Suffolk. Wonder what value the Post Office place on that?

Collecting boxes are often put into the walls of private houses. 'Does the owner get any recompense from the Post Office?' wondered a Cornish reader, 'Fraid not, not even a free book of stamps.

Dead letter boxes

Another point about pillar boxes occurred to a London motorist. Although he had seen many signposts, lamp standards, bollards and other street 'furniture' demolished by vehicles, he couldn't recall ever seeing a pillar box similarly damaged. Did we have any casualty figures? Yes, on average, one pillar box a week is victim of a traffic accident. And about forty of them are written off every year and have to be replaced. No doubt the vehicles responsible are write-offs too.

Such accidents are a matter of concern to the Letter Box Study Group. The Liverpool Special was an 1863 model of which only six were made, for the city of Liverpool. Three years ago only three were left. Then, horror of horrors, an Army lorry reversed into one. So, to save the species from extinction the Group persuaded the Post Office to transplant one out of harm's way outside the new Liverpool Head Post Office.

Hopping mad

We don't know what the Group's attitude was to George Corner, of Batley, Yorks, a man who had a healthy disrespect for the objects of their devotion. For years he indulged in his self-styled sport of 'wogglehopping' – leap-frogging over pillar boxes to raise money for handicapped children. He once made a round-Britain tour during which he hopped over 1,000 boxes. And at the age of seventy-seven he took delivery of his very own Victorian pillar box – how much he paid for it remains a secret. George finally retired from wogglehopping, having cleared his last post box one month after his seventy-ninth birthday.

The design of pillar boxes over which George hopped is a hundred years old. It first appeared in 1879 but for some curious reason, between then and 1887, boxes had no Royal cipher nor even the words 'Post Office' on them. Consequently, boxes of that period – and there were still about 580 in use – are known to enthusiasts as 'anonymous'.

Post prandial

From time to time we Old Pair receive mildly mauled envelopes on which apologetic postmasters have written cryptic notes like 'damaged by snails'. At first we thought this had something to do with the speed of delivery, but apparently snails have a taste for the gum on envelopes and postage stamps and lurk in pillar boxes waiting for their favourite nosh to be delivered to them. So bad is the problem in some areas that pillar boxes are treated with pellets to kill the gourmet gastropods.

Receiving end
Having dealt with collecting boxes, for the benefit of postmen we ought to point out that the letter box in your front door should, ideally, be placed 3ft 6ins from the ground and the opening be at least 10ins by 1½ins.

The postman's job would be a lot easier, too, if we all used our postcode. This system was first tried out as a pilot scheme in Norwich in 1959, but the improved system commenced officially in Croydon in 1966 and was completed in 1974, with Norwich being recoded. Today there are one and a half million postcodes.

The numbering of London postal districts was introduced in 1917 to help the unskilled postal sorters employed during the First World War.

Delivery dates
How long since postmen delivered on Sunday mornings? Not since June 12, 1921. And when did we last have a delivery on Christmas Day? In England, Wales and Northern Ireland, in 1960; in Scotland, in 1965. The first Christmas card was designed for and sent by Sir Henry Cole in 1843. Sir Henry was a man of many parts. A top civil servant who supported Rowland Hill's reform of the Post Office, he also helped promote the Great Exhibition of 1851 and was largely responsible for founding the Victoria and Albert Museum, the Albert Hall, and the Royal College of Music. As if that weren't enough, under the pen-name Felix Summerly he wrote children's books and guidebooks.

His Christmas card idea must have been worth millions to the Post Office. By 1879 eleven million of them were being sent and ninety-nine years later the figure was around the 461 million mark.

Homing device
Three sailors wrote to us many moons ago to ask if it were true that a drunken man could walk into a post office and get himself posted home. Ever ready to oblige the customers – or get out of the office for ten minutes – our lad George went

down to the post office to see if he could get himself delivered back to us. He returned soberly, having been informed that that is something the Post Office will not do for drunken sailors, cheeky office boys or anyone else! They used to have a Conducted Persons Service which was chiefly used by people in a strange town looking for a particular address. It was part of the telegraph boy's job to conduct them to the correct address. But that service was suspended in January, 1952.

Postage due

Another misconception we are sometimes asked to correct is that letters to Postmasters, Members of Parliament, or to Government departments may be posted without stamp. All such correspondence should be prepaid just as if it were addressed to a private person. Only those envelopes with the Official Post design provided by the Post Office or Government departments may be posted without postage stamp. The only other exceptions are addresses or petitions to Her Majesty the Queen or to either House of Parliament, which may be posted free of charge.

But what is a valid postage stamp? A couple of years ago a reader was annoyed because a relative had to pay 'Postage Due' on a letter on which he had stuck a King George VI stamp. 'I'm sure,' he said, 'that stamps from the previous monarch's reign are valid.' That may have been the practice formerly, but now only decimal postage stamps are valid. With the exception of the £1 values, even £sd stamps of Elizabeth's reign are invalid.

The £15,000 fiddle

Although at the start of each year, as a small service to stamp collectors, we publish a list of the new British stamps to be issued during the year, the subject of stamps in themselves is too vast and specialised for us to go into here. But it is worth recording that, so far as is known, only one British stamp has been forged in order to defraud the Post Office.

In 1898, a stamp collector named Charles Nissen noticed that some of his one-shilling stamps of 1872 issue had no watermark. An official enquiry disclosed that for some months during 1872-73, a clerk in the telegraph office at

London's Stock Exchange had been forging the stamps, which were bought mainly by brokers sending telegrams to their clients. It was estimated that the clerk had made some £15,000 by this fraud but by the time Nissen discovered it the clerk was already dead and he was never named.

Rings a bell

We could hardly take leave of the Post Office without mentioning the other great side of their organisation, telecommunications. Britain's system of telephones, telex connections and data transmission terminals is the third largest in the world after the United States and Japan. It's the telephone, naturally, which most interests our readers. After all, there are 23,000,000 of them – telephones, that is – and last year between us we made some 17,454,000,000 calls, 14,600,000,000 of 'em local, 2,703,000,000 trunk and 151,000,000 international.

All that after only a hundred years of development. For it was in 1878 that Alexander Graham Bell demonstrated his electronic speaking instrument to Queen Victoria at Osborne, Isle of Wight. A year later, London's first telephone exchange was opened at Lombard Street with ten subscribers, who paid a fixed charge of £20 a year for all calls, plus a rent of £7 for each mile of wire used!

Quicker by bike

An old sports reporter once asked us to clear up something which had been puzzling him for years. He distinctly remembered reporting a Saturday afternoon soccer match in 1904. The game was three miles from his newspaper's offices in Bristol and he rode an old push bike those three miles with the first-half 'copy', returning to the game to get the result and so back to the office. All for the princely sum of 2s 6d. What puzzled him was, if the telephone system was then in use, why didn't he use it?

Well, Bristol certainly had the telephone in those days, but public call boxes weren't introduced until 1908, when some sixty or seventy kiosks were set up, the charge being 2d a call. Kiosk number one was in Nottingham and number two in Folkestone, the latter being a very fancy affair made to resemble a hexagonal rustic arbour with wooden filigree-work!

At that time the system was still owned by the National Telephone Company. The Government bought control of the company in 1911 and handed it over to the General Post Office two years later.

Camouflaged kiosks

Although, so far as we know, nothing so fancy as that original Folkestone kiosk still exists, readers occasionally ask us about the odd green telephone box they find, usually in country places. Kiosks can be painted green, or dark grey, to harmonise with their natural surroundings, at the request of local councils and when recommended by the Royal Fine Arts Commission. However, London's only green kiosk – at Savoy Place, off the Thames Embankment – was painted thus because it was erected, in February 1928, on the property of the Institute of Electrical Engineers, which gave permission for the kiosk only on that condition.

Vandals rule OK?

The great drawback with telephone kiosks is that they are so vulnerable to the attentions of vandals, a problem which cost £1,352,000 in 1978 and is a constant challenge to the ingenuity of Post Office engineers – and many of our readers. One chap, frustrated on finding that every call box in the area had had its light bulb smashed or removed, wondered why boxes aren't fitted with luminous dials. Such a dial can be fitted to certain private 'phones, but the Post Office considers that for public call boxes the provision of a normal electric light bulb should be adequate in a civilised country.

And we must say we can see their point. Apart from the enormous cost (there are 78,000 public telephone kiosks), luminous dials would be an admission of defeat to the vandals and petty thieves.

Another anti-vandal suggestion from a reader was to fit a coin box to the door mechanism. Then to get into the kiosk one would have to pay a nominal charge which would also pay for the first local call. This seemed a reasonable idea to us, but the Post Office pointed out objections which make the idea impracticable. In the first place it would disrupt the 999 emergency call service, which must be freely available with the minimum delay. And again the cost of a mechanism which would open the door and give one free call but no more would be prohibitive.

Quick on the dial . . .

Come to think of it – and readers often do – why was 999 chosen as the emergency number? Surely 111 would be quicker to dial?

No doubt it would, but at the time the emergency dialling system was introduced, in 1937, the number 111 tended to send an unreliable signal. 222, which is also a quicker number to dial, was rejected as a national signal because in London it connected with the old Abbey exchange. The objection to 000, which is easier to find in the dark, is that it is indistinguishable in an emergency from an ordinary call to the exchange operator.

And now, after all these years of dialling 999, it would be impossible to re-educate the public to a new emergency number.

At the third stroke

Even older than the 999 service is the speaking clock, which started in 1936. Despite the introduction of other recorded information services, such as 'Dial a Disc', weather forecasts, bedtime stories, cricket scores, the share index, the telephone time check remains the most used, clocking up around 400 million calls every year. Still popularly known as TIM, from the days when 'phone dials had letters as well as numbers, the clock's voice was originally that of Jane Cane but since 1963 has been that of Miss Pat Simmons. Pat retired in 1976 after thirty-nine years with the Post Office, for which she was awarded the Imperial Service Medal.

Another money spinner is the alarm call: 7,500,000 such calls were made in 1978, at a cost to the sleepy heads of £1,790,000.

Crossed lines

The Subscriber Trunk Dialling system was inaugurated by the Queen on December 5, 1958, by calling up the Lord Provost of Edinburgh from Bristol.

We must admit that since we started dialling our own calls, or let Lottie dial 'em, we seem to get an awful lot of wrong numbers, which we must get charged for since, unlike an exchange operator, the automatic equipment can't make allowances for them.

A similar bone of contention is the infernal crossed line, the incidence of which also appeared to increase with direct dialling. The Post Office once told us, in answer to a reader's query, that when we get a crossed line we don't have to pay for it because the call has already been charged to one of the other parties talking. But having published that official reasurance we received the following letter signed by 'Ten Post Office Engineers', who wrote from South-West London:

'We were absolutely appalled by the misleading information supplied to you by the Post Office to the effect that if you dial a number and get a crossed line it doesn't cost you anything at all.

'Metering of a call starts as soon as the called subscriber answers. When a call switches to an existing conversation this metering condition is already in existence and the "intruder" will also be charged. And, as you Old Pair pointed out, you also get charged for wrong numbers.

'Either of these faults should be reported to the engineers and a call to the operator will enable your call to be extended to its proper destination, with an allowance made for the mischarged call.'

So now you know.

Ring of untruth

We got another bum steer when we were asked to confirm that if a telephone is left off the hook for a long time it will explode. Declining to make the experiment ourselves, we again asked for the authorised version and were told that a telephone left off the hook for a longish period won't explode but it will certainly blow a fuse at the exchange. The time taken to do this, as our informant said, depended on the loading on the circuits. To us strictly non-technical Old Pair, that sounded too technical not to be true.

Alas, we'd been too trusting again. Mr G. Robertson, BSc, Assistant Executive Engineer at the Post Office Telecommunications HQ, put us right:

'What actually happens is basically thus: if a 'phone is left off the hook for longer than about a minute, an automatic release is effected and dial tone ceases. If the condition is brought to the attention of engineering staff in the exchange, a "graduated howler" can be used to attract the attention of the subscriber.

'This noise, becoming louder and louder, can easily give the impression that something drastic is about to happen.'

Even if we are not at risk of being blown up by our telephones, some folk worry about the risk of infection from telephone mouthpieces. One lady, having been told that ordinary disinfectant may damage the instrument, asked what should be used. The solution is cetrimide BP, which can be obtained at most chemists – a very weak one of about a teaspoonful to a gallon of water. And having washed your mouthpiece out, let's hope you will never be accused of coprophonia – the technical term for using obscene language on the blower!

You have been warned

Actually you can find yourself in telephone trouble with the Post Office for an offence which, we suspect, many people commit in total ignorance of the law. Indeed, we Old Pair once recommended the 'crime' as a good idea! A reader told us how she had rigged up a toy telephone connection to the house of an elderly neighbour to be used in case of emergency. H. Stott, of Stapleford Abbots, Essex, then pointed out that strictly speaking this was against the law:

'All communications by Electric Wires or Radiation are the monopoly of the Post Office Corporation under the current Telegraphy and Wireless Telegraphy Acts, effective (and updated periodically) since the mid-1840s.

'These cover all messages or signals by speech or code and all signalling including bells. Only Railway, Canal and Military Authorities are not covered by the Acts, which have been held to cover (and prohibit public use of) light-rays and all invisible rays for all signalling or messaging.

'The monopoly is for messaging/signalling between or over separately-owned premises. I am advised that only a mechanical signal (pull-wire or string) or soundwaves – hand-bell or drum – are outside the monopoly, the extent of which is staggering.

'The public gave up their rights to the Government before they knew what they were surrendering.'

We're pretty sure that in the case of the good neighbour the Post Office would turn a deaf ear, as it were, but their exclusive rights in that respect are worth remembering.

With certain exceptions, the Post Office also has the exclusive right to carry letters. Broadly speaking letters may be sent by a private friend, or an employee, and letters appertaining to goods can be delivered by the carrier of the goods. But carriers cannot carry letters alone nor, especially, can anyone other than the Post Office collect letters for delivery.

They've got a motto

But let's not end on a stern note. We Old Pair always delight in the apt quotation and we reckon there can be no more fitting motto for a Post Office than these lines from the Greek historian, Herodotus:

> *Neither snow, nor rain, nor heat, nor gloom of night stays these couriers from the swift completion of their appointed rounds.*

Alas, the Yanks got there before us – the quote is inscribed on the New York Post Office. Our own Post Office's motto is the rather more prosaic Latin: 'Cura Fide Studio', which translated means Service, Sincerity and Diligence. By and large, we reckon they live up to it.

BRIDGING THE GAP

WE were once asked if it was true that there is a bridge which crosses the Atlantic. Incredibly enough, there is. It connects the Island of Seil, on the west coast of Scotland, with the Argyll mainland. The bridge spans the Clachan Sound which is part of the Atlantic Ocean.

While jogging our memories on that particular query by dipping into our Little Black Book, we found that much water had flowed under our personal bridges during the years in which we have been answering readers' questions on the subject generally. This chapter endeavours to tap some of the stream of inquiries. Some deal with entirely factual matters; others provide anecdotes which are themselves footnotes to history.

For a start, a definition. Everyone knows that a bridge crosses water. But what, we've been asked, differentiates it from a viaduct? The latter has a much more restricted meaning, referring to a structure which spans a valley.

London bridges

Now, some queries on Thames spanners. When was Battersea Bridge opened? The Earl of Rosebery did the honours on Monday, July 21, 1890.

Is it true (asked a Swindon reader) that they used to test bridges over the Thames by means of a bundle of straw suspended from the centre of the arches?

No. The custom originated as a warning to users of a waterway that a bridge is under repair. It is not confined to the Thames.

The longest and the lowest

What is the longest bridge over the Thames and which is the lowest? The longest is Waterloo which is 2,456ft in length.

The answer to which is the lowest is slightly more difficult. Depends on what you mean, as philosopher Joad used to remark. In one way it is Hammersmith Bridge, in another it isn't. On the tidal Thames, that is up to Teddington Lock, Hammersmith is indeed the lowest, being 14ft 3ins above high water level. But above Teddington, on the non-tidal Thames, the lowest bridge is at Osney, Oxford, normally 7ft 7ins above water level.

Mention of Hammersmith puts us in mind of a letter we

received from Irene Littlejohns, of Bishop Auckland, Co. Durham. She informed us that she possessed an heirloom, a stone wine flask, inscribed 'W. Bacchus, Wine and Brandy Merchant, Suspension Bridge Inn, Hammersmith'. She asked if we knew anything about it.

A little. The Inn – named after London's first suspension bridge – was built on the site of the Goat Inn, pulled down in 1826. In the past century, the inn has had three name changes – first the City Arms, then the Harlequin, and in 1978, the Old City Arms.

W. Bacchus, it is thought, was the first landlord of the Suspension Bridge Inn. Aptly named, at least, for a dispenser of the products of the grape!

Out of step

Two Camberwell readers, 'Bill and George', had a wager involving ten 'gaspers' over the question: 'When large squads of troops march over London's bridges, are they ordered to fall out of step in case the vibrations from the stamp of heavy boots cause damage?'

The answer's negative, since London bridges aren't affected – nor are any others (in normal conditions) except suspension ones. On them, the order is given 'Break Step!' Otherwise the bridge might swing with possibly disastrous results. Bridges supported by pillars aren't affected.

Landmark

Probably the most famous landmark on the London scene is Tower Bridge, featured in countless millions of postcards and other mementoes the world over. Naturally, we've had numerous requests for information about it.

To kick off, a common question is: 'How true is it that Tower Bridge is lifted hydraulically by one quart of water?' Not true. The movable spans – or bascules – are balanced like see-saws on pivots, with 442 tons of ballast at each end where they join the fixed part of the bridge. When the hydraulic system lifts the bridge, tons, not quarts of water are used. The water comes from tanks and is used over and over again. Approximately, only one quart is lost during each lift, which is, no doubt, how the fallacy arose.

Designer

Tower Bridge was designed by Sir Horace Jones and Sir J. Wolfe Barry. It was completed in 1894 at a cost of one million pounds. The original hydraulic engines were supplied by Armstrong Mitchell, though there have been many modifications and renovations over the years.

Leap to it!

Still on Tower Bridge, we were asked a year or two back if a double-decker was ever driven through the air to clear the gap as it opened for shipping. It's no phoney story. At 9.35 pm on December 31, 1952, a number 78 bus from Dalston to Peckham was near the middle of Tower Bridge when it began to open.

The driver, Albert Gunter, with great presence of mind, accelerated and the bus jumped the gap of some three feet to land safely on the other side of the bridge. Twelve of the passengers on board were treated for shock – as were the two crew. Driver Gunter received a £10 reward . . . and no doubt some grateful handshakes, even if they weren't exactly golden ones.

Daredevil

Vague memories linger on among some readers of the first man to fly a plane under Tower Bridge. One or two plumped for Lieutenant Butler, of the Royal Navy, who is reputed to have flipped beneath sometime during the First World War. However, the honour, according to our LBB, goes to Sir Frank Kennedy McClean, father of naval aviation, who flew a biplane under the bridge in 1911 or 1912. Can't, unfortunately, be more specific.

Stunt failed

Sir Frank was far from being the only person to use Tower Bridge as a scene for a stunt. He survived, but others weren't so lucky. Shortly after the bridge was opened on June 30, 1894, it hit the headlines because of a dive to death.

A stunt man, Ben Fuller, plunging from the overhead footpath, 142ft above high water, was killed. After that the footpath was fenced in, and eventually it was closed altogether. It is alleged that the reason was to prevent people from committing suicide, but it's more likely that the cost of maintaining lifts, etc., made it a dead loss in another sense!

Raise it!

A Welling, Kent, reader asked us a double-barrelled question. How do ships sailing up the Thames indicate that they wish to pass through Tower Bridge, and do they pay a special toll? The answers are that they show they want to pass through by flying a ball and pennant, and they don't have to pay a toll. The money for operating the bridge comes from rents of the Corporation of the City of London.

Sic transit gloria!

Every child knows the rhyme 'London Bridge is falling down' – a perfectly true comment, as it happens, of the old one opened by King William and Queen Adelaide in 1831. Despite repeated attempts to strengthen it, it became so dangerous that in the last decade it was dismantled stone by stone, and 12,000 separately numbered pieces of granite were shipped across the Atlantic to Lake Havasu City in Arizona. They were re-assembled over an artificial water-channel named, appropriately enough, 'Little Thames'.

For the record, the bridge was snapped up by a subsidiary of the McCulloch Oil Corporation of California for a cool £1 million. The new London Bridge was opened in 1973. It was designed by Harold Knox King, who worked for the City of London Corporation for 25 years, the last ten as City Engineer. It cost £5 million pounds, paid out of Bridge House Estates, i.e., the tolls, rents and benefactions of former Londoners.

Suspension

The Clifton suspension bridge over the Avon gorge at Bristol has, over the years, been the subject of numerous inquiries from our readers. One that crops up regularly is whether this bridge at one time spanned the Thames. Although the answer is no, it's not such an odd-ball question as it might at first appear. What happened is that the designer, Brunel, used, in its construction in 1864, chains from the old Hungerford suspension bridge which spanned the Thames at Charing Cross and which was dismantled in 1860.

Another question we've been asked is about the height of the Clifton Bridge. It is 245ft above high water level. And its length? 702ft. In reply to a reader who wanted to know how this compared with the Severn Bridge, the answer is that the latter is 3,240ft long, with two side spans of 1,000ft each.

Parachuted!

An Oxford reader wanted to know if it was true that a young lady once tried to commit suicide by jumping from the Clifton Bridge but was saved by her crinoline which acted as a parachute. Absolutely true. The young lady was Sarah Ann Henley who, in 1885, after a quarrel with her lover, said goodbye to all that and threw herself off. Poor Sarah Ann – or rather lucky Sarah Ann – was sustained by her crinoline and landed, unscathed, in the mud below. Presumably, after that experience, her falls were confined to men, for she lived to the ripe old age of eighty-five, dying in 1948!

The story of Sarah Ann reminded us of other examples of free fall jumps without a chute. A few years ago an American stunt man deliberately dropped thousands of feet before being handed a chute in mid-air by another member of his acrobatic team. And during the last war there are several accounts of airmen surviving jumps without a parachute by landing in a snow-clad tree or haystack which broke their fall. But the petticoat parachutist has a unique niche in the history of unlikely survivals!

Incidentally, some years ago when we were looking into the subject of violent deaths and their connection, if any, with ghost stories, we were surprised at the number of suicides committed over the years, particularly last century, by people jumping off the Clifton Bridge. It seems to have had a fatal fascination, attracting unfortunates not merely from far afield in Britain but even from abroad.

Prank

More recently the Clifton Bridge hit the headlines when some adventurous lads from Oxford University jumped off at the end of rubber ropes – giving a new meaning to suspension! They bounced merrily up and down until hauled to safety and a wigging from the beak! Their joke produced a bumper crop of puns such as 'No point in sending them down – they'd be sure to be sprung!' Ouch!

Towering

Among further questions we've received about other bridges in Britain are these:

Q. Is Yorkshire's Skelton Grange 'B' power station taller than the Firth of Forth road bridge towers?

A. No. The 512ft towers of the Forth Bridge top Skelton Grange 'B' by 12ft.

Q. What is the length of the Forth road bridge?

A. Some 6,000ft. The main span has a length of 3,300ft.

Q. Which railway bridge spans the wider stretch of water – the Forth or the Tay?

A. The Tay. Its total length is 11,653ft of which 10,289ft is over the estuary. The Forth railway bridge is 8,295ft long.

Q. Which is higher – the Clifton suspension bridge or Newcastle-upon-Tyne high level bridge?

A. The former wins by 82ft.

In suspense

Q. Was Thomas Telford's bridge across the Menai Strait to Anglesey the world's first suspension one?

A. By no means. The Chinese were building suspension bridges 400 years before the birth of Christ. The principle was revived in Italy during the Renaissance of the sixteenth century and again in America in the early 1800s.

Q. The Tyne Bridge at Newcastle-upon-Tyne and the Sydney Harbour Bridge, Australia, are identical. Which is the copy?

A. The Newcastle bridge was opened in 1928, the Sydney one in 1932. Both were constructed by the Middlesbrough firm, Dorman Long.

Relic

Q. Which is the oldest bridge in Britain?

A. It's usually reckoned to be the bridge known as the Tarr Steps, over the River Barle on Exmoor, Somerset. Built of massive boulders and slabs, it is believed to date from before 500 BC.

Q. What are Gerber Bridges?

A. What we now call cantilever bridges – ones in which the

arms project from the piers and connect in the middle of the span. The term cantilever was first used about 1883 when the Forth Railway Bidge was being constructed on this principle. Gerbers got their name from Heinrich Gerber, the engineer who built the 524ft-long bridge at Hassfurt am Main, Germany, in 1867.

Disastrous

'Praise the bridge that carried you over,' wrote George Colman (1762-1831), a poet and dramatist. The vast majority are so soundly constructed that we take their safety for granted – but when things go wrong, the consequences are generally catastrophic. We have in our Little Black Book inquiries about two disasters – one at Staplehurst, Kent, and the other, the Tay Bridge disaster.

A loss to letters

A reader who vaguely remembered somewhere that a great writer had once been involved in a railway bridge tragedy asked if our LBB could cast any light on the matter. It could.

The writer was Charles Dickens, that great Victorian novelist; the bridge was the Beult Viaduct, built on cast-iron girders ten feet above a muddy stream near Staplehurst, Kent. The train involved was the Folkestone Boat Express, and the date was June 9, 1865.

The 32 timber baulks of the viaduct on which the rails were laid were being replaced, and the foreman of the gang, John Benge, proposed to finish the job between the passing of an uptrain at 2.51 and a down train at 4.15 on the fatal afternoon. He had misread the schedule to which the Boat Express ran. The Express was known as the 'tidal' train because it was timed to connect with the Folkestone packets. Benge thought the train was not due until after five o'clock, whilst, in fact, it thundered along at fifty miles an hour just after 3 pm.

Benge made another mistake. Instead of posting the man with the red flag 1,000 yards from the viaduct, he had him at 554 yards which did not give the driver time to draw up. Miraculously, the locomotive, its tender and leading brake van crossed the rail-less gap on the timber baulks; the first coach, in which Dickens was travelling, hung poised over the void; but as the girders collapsed, the other five coaches plunged into the stream. Ten passengers died, 49 were injured.

At the time of the accident, Dickens was reading through the manuscript of *Our Mutual Friend* to which he added a postcript, part of which reads: 'I remember with devout thankfulness that I can never be much nearer parting company with my readers for ever than I was then, until there shall be written against my life the two words with which I have this day closed this book – The End.'

Dickens scarred

The novelist escaped physical injury, but his nervous system was shattered. He subsequently commented: 'I am curiously weak, weak as if I were recovering from a long illness. I begin to feel it more in my head. I sleep well and eat well; but I write half a dozen words and turn faint and sick.'

It was some time before he could bring himself to travel on a train again, and even then he preferred slow ones. When a locomotive got up speed, he described the experience as 'inexpressibly distressing'.

Five years to the day of the disaster, Dickens died at the age of 58. Although the major cause of the stroke he suffered was undoubtedly the stress of the hectic lecturing tours he inflicted on himself in his last years, his friend and biographer, John Forster, records that the Staplehurst disaster contributed to his early end – and deprived us of the solution to his last work, *The Mystery of Edwin Drood.*

Tay Bridge Disaster

Second chronologically, of the disasters we have referred to, but the one which etched itself most deeply on the public imagination was the collapse of the old Tay Bridge on the night of Sunday, 28 December, 1879.

The bridge had been commissioned in 1871, the contract going to Messrs de Bergh & Co., and it was designed by Thomas Bouch. After three years' work, the contract was transferred to Messrs Hopkins, Gilkes & Co., and the bridge was completed in 1878. Dundee's master of bathetic doggerel, William McGonagall, celebrated the engineering feat but, in a curiously prophetic way, prayed that no ill would befall the structure. He wrote:

Beautiful Railway Bridge of the Silvery Tay!
I hope that God will protect all passengers
By night and by day,
And that no accident will befall them when crossing
The Bridge of the Silvery Tay,
For that would be most awful to be seen
Near Dundee and the Magdalen Green.

Design faults

McGonagall's prayer, unfortunately, was not to be answered on the fateful night just over a year later – partly because of an Act of God, but mainly because of design and construction faults in the bridge.

The original design was for a single line girder bridge, built on brick piers, with each span 200ft. However, this assumed that the bridge would be built on a rock foundation. When it was found that the river bed was not solid enough, Bouch, to reduce the weight on the foundations, abandoned brick piers (only 14 were used) and turned to cast-iron columns. The main spans were extended to 245ft with the exception of two of 227ft.

The bridge was constructed on a gentle gradient, and at its top point, shipping had 88ft clearance above the high water mark. From pier 41 to pier 28 the famous 'High Girders' were used. Their lower booms were on a level with the upper booms of the rest of the bridge, and the rails were laid within them instead of on top. It was the collapse of these girders which caused the disaster, in which some ninety people died.

Before the bridge was opened, it was inspected by Major-General Hutchinson of the Board of Trade. He passed it, but recommended a speed restriction on it of 25 mph. He also said he would like to test the effects of a high wind when a train of carriages ran over it. Tragically, he got his answer the following year. Queen Victoria crossed the bridge soon after it opened, and knighted Thomas Bouch for designing what was then the longest bridge in the world.

A night to remember

On the night of the disaster the train taking passengers from Edinburgh to Dundee was pulled by locomotive 224, a splendid two inside cylinder express engine and the forerunner of a type later to become common on British railways. The driver was David Mitchell, a shining example of the old-time footplate man. Not only did he see that his locomotive was immaculate; he himself wore for his shift moleskin breeches and a tailcoat.

That night there was a fierce gale blowing up the Tay, and the High Girders were unable to withstand its force, especially as they were already subjected to the weight of the train. Shortly after seven o'clock, the train plunged into the waters, trapped in the wreckage of the girders. The only immediate indication of the tragedy was a cascade of sparks, but at least one witness thought this was merely the fireman clearing his box. It was three months before the locomotive was recovered, virtually intact, with only its chimney, cab and dome casing lost, and the footplate buckled.

A committee of inquiry found that the bracing ties of the bridge and the cast iron lugs to which they were secured were defective. It apportioned most of the blame to Sir Thomas Bouch, commenting that the bridge was 'badly designed, badly constructed and badly maintained'. To this day, a memorial to the dead exists in the form of stumps which, at low water, can be seen protruding several feet in the air near the new bridge.

A 'poetic' memorial

Another memorial survives – an effusion by William McGonagall (1830-1902), who was wont to describe himself 'Poet and Tragedian'. Certainly he had an eye for the tragic though most of his readers found his renditions comic. Here is part of the last stanza of 'The Tay Bridge Disaster':

Oh! ill-fated Bridge of the Silvery Tay,
I must now conclude my lay
By telling the world fearlessly without the least dismay,
That your central girders would not have given way,
At least many sensible men do say,
Had they been supported on each side by buttresses,
At least many sensible men confesses,
For the stronger we our houses do build,
The less chance we have of being killed.

McGonagall completed his hat-trick on the Tay Bridge with an address to the new one which strikes a more optimistic note about its chances of survival:

Beautiful new railway bridge of the Silvery Tay,
With your strong brick piers and buttresses in so grand array,
And your thirteen central girders, which seem to my eye
Strong enough all storms to defy . . .

Happily, the bridge looks good for many years to come.

Track record

The dangers of incorporating cast-iron girders in bridges were well enough realised last century, but it was only after a non-fatal accident on the Brighton line in May, 1891, when a bridge constructed in this way collapsed near Norwood Junction, that something was done about them. The Board of Trade Inspector, Major-General Hutchinson, recommended the replacement of all cast-iron girders with wrought iron or steel girders. His recommendation was implemented.

The railways in Britain have, in fact, had a remarkable safety record, and even accidents involving bridges, built as they used to be of unreliable materials – timber or cast-iron – were comparatively rare. Where the bridges were made of brick or wrought iron, such as Brunel's one over the Thames at Maidenhead, they have stood the test of time.

In the standard book on rail accidents, *Red for Danger,* the author, L. T. C. Rolt, lists only eight involving bridges between 1846, when the first occurred, and 1925, the last (so far as we can see) to be caused either by faulty design or freak weather conditions. For the record, the 1846 accident occurred between Tonbridge and Penshurst station in Kent, when the River Medway, in full spate, carried away part of a timber trestle bridge. The train, tender and leading wagons of an up night goods train fell through the gap. The fireman got his injured driver out of the wreckage, but the latter died soon after.

Historic bridges

Now a section on historic bridges which have featured in our correspondence column or in private answers to readers. Possibly the most famous bridge in history – or, more accurately, myth-history – was Rome's Sulpician Bridge. It was celebrated in ancient lays, and in modern times in a ballad by Macaulay, as the scene of the battle where Horatius and two comrades held the whole Etruscan army at bay. We were asked for details such as the names of the comrades.

Horatius Cocles (meaning the 'one-eyed') was accompanied by Spurius Lartius and Titus Herminius, while the Etruscan army was led by Lars Porsena. According to the Roman version of events (a totally false one) Horatius and his two braves held off the enemy while the bridge was broken down behind them, thus cutting off an attack on Rome. As the tale has it, when the bridge was almost hewn through, Horatius sent his companions back and fought on until it collapsed. He then plunged into the water and swam to safety. So grateful were the Romans that they raised a statue to him and allowed him as much land as he could plough in a day.

The only trouble with this tale of superhuman prowess is that it is complete hocus-pocus, a romantic fabrication designed to cover up one of the most serious defects the Romans suffered in their early history. Far from Rome being saved, it was completely conquered by Lars Porsena, the Romans acknowledging their subjugation by presenting him with a sceptre, a royal robe, and an ivory chair. Porsena underlined their humiliation by forcing them to beat their swords into ploughshares. So much for historical 'fact'!

Poetic record

Anyway, as has been remarked, it is all right raping history providing you have a child by her. Macaulay's *Lays of Ancient Rome* presumably qualify on these grounds, and of the *Lays,* the most famous is his ballad *Horatius* which generations of schoolkids groaned their way through:

With weeping and with laughter
Still is the story told,
How well Horatius kept the bridge
In the brave days of old.

Incidentally, the ballad contains one of the best known couplets in the English language. Describing the Etruscan attack on the bridge, Macaulay writes:

But those behind cried 'forward'
And those before cried 'back'.

Old crossings

Other historic bridges we have been asked about include the Roman one at Alcantara, Spain, the Bridge of Sighs in Venice, and the Peschiera, in Italy. And one of our precocious schoolboy readers tried to have us on by inquiring the where- abouts of the Pons Asinorum, the Bridge of Asses. It isn't, of course, a bridge at all, but refers to the fifth proposition of the first book of Euclid's geometry which many beginners found so difficult that they didn't attempt to pass on to even tougher mathematical concepts!

As for the bridge at Alcantara, it spans the River Tagus, and was built in AD 105. It is 131ft high and 670ft long, and is a beautiful example of Roman design at its best.

The Bridge of Sighs (Ponte dei Sospiri) connects the Ducal Palace in Venice to the prison. It was the prospect of executionor incarceration which occasioned the sighs! The bridge was built by Rizzo some time between 1483 and 1498.

Incidentally, it is mentioned in Byron's poem *Childe Harold,* where he records:

I stood in Venice, on the Bridge of Sighs;
A palace and a prison on each hand.

Another bridge which features in a poem by the Victorian writer, A. H. Clough, is the Peschiera. Of it he wrote:

What voice did on my spirit fall,
Peschiera, when thy bridge I crost.

The bridge he refers to is at Peschiera di Garda, on Lake Garda, northern Italy. This is near the point where the River Mincio flows out of the lake to join up eventually with the Po and so on to the Adriatic.

Wartime bridges

But not all the bridges we've been asked about are ancient ones. Modern times have thrown up some famous ones also, and the last war, in particular, saw three at least pass into history. They are the Bridge over the River Kwai, the Pegasus Bridge in Normandy, and that 'Bridge Too Far' at Arnhem.

Earlier this year, a reader's letter prompted us to have a look at the truth or fiction behind the Kwai Bridge. Pat Summers of Sedgwick, near Kendal, Cumbria, told us that, while on holiday in Thailand, she and her husband visited Kanchanaburi, site of the bridge. The Allied war cemeteries, she said, were beautifully looked after, with as many flowers as possible which resembled English ones. She commented: 'It did seem like a small piece of England forever in a foreign field.'

Naturally, we printed her letter for the sake of readers who lost loved ones in those bloody Burmese battles. Then we had a look around to see what we could dig up about the bridge . . .

For a start, it was a section of the 250 mile-railway from Thailand to Burma which, in a period of fourteen months between 1942 and 1943, was built under the orders, and guns, of the Japanese. More than 100,000 people, including 16,000 prisoners of war, died during its construction from diseases such as beri-beri, starvation, and heat exhaustion. We asked a Japanese journalist working nowadays in London about this. He simply shrugged his shoulders and commented:'You westerners place too high a value on life. Thousands of Japanese died in the building of the Burmese railway, and officers drove their men as hard as they drove the prisoners.'

A second point is that three bridges were, in fact, built over the Kwai. Two were wooden ones and did not survive. The third, the one featured in the film based on Pierre Boulle's novel, is made of steel and most of the original structure is intact, though three of the spans were destroyed by Allied bombing in 1945, and replaced after the war. The story that POWs working for British intelligence planted explosives under the bridge to destroy it is pure fiction, but it gives the plot more tension than a standard air raid!

Today, the bridge is a major tourist attraction, with nearby restaurants, souvenir shops, and local song-and-dance troupes catering for a motley throng of visitors. Death, where is thy sting, and commerce, where thy victory?

Winged horse

'Pegasus' – the winged horse of Greek mythology – was the name given to one of the bridges over the River Orne, in Normandy, which the airborne forces had to capture on D-Day. They took all five on their operational list, intact, although they were primed for destruction. The paras also destroyed all crossings of the nearby River Dives, to prevent a German counter-attack. Finally, on the same day, they blasted their way into the Merville fortress, which was firing directly on the beaches. To do so, they had to storm through a minefield which took a heavy toll. Their commander, Colonel Otway, received the VC. The operation is described in Chester Wilmot's book, *The Struggle for Europe.*

Wilmot, an Australian journalist, went in on D-Day in one of the gliders, and filed on the rest of the war from the angle of a correspondent working alongside Monty's forces.

Sadly, he was killed in a Comet crash over the Mediterranean while on a peacetime mission. But his book is still an enthralling read.

A bridge too far

The third of the bridges we have mentioned – at Arnhem – is famous as inspiring the book *A Bridge Too Far* by Cornelius Ryan and the film based on it. Situated on the Lower Rhine, in Holland, it was the fifth crucial bridge which had to be taken intact by the airborne troops of the Allies if the ground attack aimed at the industrial heart of Germany was to succeed. Many of our readers took part in the drop and those who survived were among the men asked by Ryan to fill in a questionnaire which helped him to flesh out his narrative with personal anecdotes and recollections. (It was, regrettably, his last book before he died of cancer.)

'Operation Market-Garden', as it was called, was intended not only to pave the way to the Ruhr, but also to Rotterdam, from where V-2s were bombarding London. Final details of the action were discussed at Field Marshal Montgomery's headquarters on September 10, 1944. Among those present was Lt-General Frederick Browning, Deputy Commander, First Allied Airborne Army, who asked, 'How long will it take the armour to reach us?' Monty replied, 'Two days.' Browning commented, 'We can hold it for four.' Then he added, 'But, sir, I think we might be going a bridge too far.'

Unfortunately, his judgment was vindicated, the operation failing partly because plans for it fell into enemy hands, partly because intelligence reports of German forces in the area, especially a Panzer division, were ignored. Browning's conduct in action could not be faulted, and it is a pity that the portrayal of his character in the film caused immense distress to his widow, novelist Daphne du Maurier.

Opinion among leaders who took part in the operation is still divided on whether or not Browning was right, and it's not the kind of controversy we Aging Contemptibles can get involved in. Our interest lies in the human stories behind such action, and we'd like to quote from a book on the making of the film, *The Arnhem Report* by Ian Johnstone (A Star Book), in which Corporal Terry Brace sums up the reaction of many of the men who took part in the fighting, some of the most savage of the war:

'The experience I had was that I got a much broader context of life. I like to think that I grew up at Arnhem. It opened my eyes. I didn't believe that one person could care so much for another person. The comradeship I saw at Arnhem was unique. People were willing to give everything: their last crumb of bread, their last drop of water, their last drop of blood. You saw the very best in humanity. This is an experience which will always be with me.'

It's good to think that, out of the blood, sweat and tears, something worth-while emerged and that Arnhem was not entirely a vain sacrifice.

De Groot's bridgehead

The final section of this chapter deals with foreign bridges which happily were never in anything more than verbal fighting. One was the Sydney Harbour Bridge, and the question we were asked was, Who opened it? We gave the technically correct answer that the official opening was performed by the then Premier of New South Wales, Mr G. T. Lang, on March 18, 1932.

However, 'Digger Ernie' wrote to us from Shoeburyness, Essex, to point out that the bridge was unofficially opened an hour previous to that ceremony by Captain De Groot, of the New Guard. He and his men had made a special trip from Melbourne to upstage the Prime Minister – and they succeeded! The Captain rode on to the bridge and cut the tape with his sword, shouting, 'I open this bridge in the name of the King.' He was dragged from his horse, and subsequently arrested and fined a fiver.

Riddle of the Kafue bridge

A London reader who had enjoyed the holiday of a lifetime on a trip through southern Africa in the sixties asked us to explain the plaque on the Kafue bridge, in Zambia, which overlooks a famous hippo pool. It says that, at one time, the bridge spanned the Thames. Our reader wanted to know if this were true.

In a sense, the answer is yes. Three spans of the old 'temporary' steel Waterloo Bridge were incorporated in the structure. We knew that they and other parts of Waterloo Bridge had been dismantled in 1943 and transported to Holland to replace bridges destroyed by the Germans. But we didn't know how they eventually got to Zambia.

A Birmingham reader came to the rescue. Mr S. Crowder informed us that a plaque in the Kafue bridge gave the additional information that it had been 'erected by the Beit Trustees out of funds bequeathed by the late Mr Alfred Beit'. That gave us the necessary clue. Mr Beit was a Jewish financier, born in Hamburg in 1853. In the 1870s he set up as a diamond merchant in Kimberley, South Africa, and later founded a similar business in London. He became a naturalised Briton and spent much of his fortune promoting British influence abroad. Mr Beit died in 1906.

The Ceylonese connection

A final question on foreign bridges – was there ever a bridge of any kind linking Ceylon and the mainland of India? Yes. Known as 'Adam's Bridge', it consisted of a chain of rocks and sandbanks 17 miles long, and was covered by only a few feet of water. It used to connect the south coast of Madras and Manar Island, off the north-west coast of Ceylon. But years ago it was dredged to let shipping through. The 'Bridge' is accepted as evidence that Ceylon was once part of the mainland.

And with that we'll cross our bridge to the next topic.

QUOTE ...MISQUOTE

'EVERY quotation,' remarked Dr Johnson, himself a dab hand at coining memorable phrases, 'contributes something to the stability or enlargement of the language.' On each weekday, except Saturday, *Live Letters* publishes a 'Thought', and this has become a popular feature with readers, some of whom use them to compile their own treasuries of quotations.

The range of material from which we can select is enormous. Indeed, when you think of it, books have been put together from the works of any one of Shakespeare, Bacon, Byron, Hazlitt, Chesterfield, Dr Johnson, Montaigne, La Rochefoucauld and others. Our aim is variety and ideas which provoke reflection. By and large we avoid cynicism, though it is often amusing, and, to avoid offending personal sensitivities, we keep clear of a partisan view of religion or politics, sticking to general observations.

We also tend to ignore strictly literary quotations such as Byron's 'I woke up and found myself famous' or Carlyle's 'A well written life is almost as rare as a well spent one.' This is because of their limited relevance to our readers. The same goes for specific historical sayings like Charles II on Nell Gwynne, 'Let not poor Nelly starve.'

In short, we aim at brief (because of shortage of space) pearls of wisdom – 'what oft was thought but ne'er so well expressed'. Here is a selection strung loosely together in the form of an alphabetical list of subjects:

Art
'A mere copier of nature can never produce anything great.' *(Sir Joshua Reynolds, 1723-1792)*

Agreements
'Covenants without the sword are but words.' *(Thomas Hobbes, 1588-1679)*

Blood sports
'Wild animals never kill for sport. Man is the only one to whom the torture and death of his fellow-creatures is amusing in itself.' *(J. A. Froude, 1818-1894)*

Breakdown
Babylon in all its desolation is a sight not so awful as that of the human mind in ruins.' *(Scrope Berdmore Davies, c. 1783-1852)*

Behaviour
Animals can be driven crazy by placing too many in too small a pen. Humans are the only animal that voluntarily does this to themselves.' *(Robert Heinlein, contemp.)*

Class
You can put flesh on a pig, but not on a thoroughbred.' *(Ida Andrews, 1927-1964)*

Cookery
Kissing don't last: cookery do!' *(George Meredith, 1828-1909)*

Corporations
Did you ever expect a corporation to have a conscience, when it has no soul to be damned, and no body to be kicked?' *(The Second Baron Thurlow, 1781-1829)*

Corruption
Nobody ever becomes totally corrupt at a stroke.' *(Juvenal, 60-c. 130)*

Courage
The following may not be the last words of the former Pakistani Prime Minister, Mr Ali Bhutto, who was hanged on 5 April, 1979, but they are his last memorable words:
A poet and a revolutionary – that is what I have been all these years. And that is how I shall remain until the last breath is gone from my body.'

Cynicism
A cynic . . . is a man who knows the price of everything and the value of nothing.' *(Oscar Wilde, 1856-1900)*

Danger
Danger, the spur of all great minds.' *(George Chapman, c. 1559-1634)*

Death

'In the midst of life we are in death.' *(Book of Commor Prayer)*

'I'm as scared of dying as anyone else. But it is the ability no to show fear which matters.' *(Airey Neave, 1916-1979).*

(Mr Neave was the Shadow Conservative spokesman or Northern Ireland and was killed by an IRA bomb in the Palace of Westminster on Friday, 30 March, 1979. His words have a particular significance in that he had a remarkable wa record, being the first British officer to escape from the Naz prison fortress, Colditz, and also winning the DSO, the MC the French Croix de Guerre, etc.)

'The claw of the seapuss gets us all in the end.' *(James Thurber, 1894-1961)*

'The most rational cure after all for the inordinate fear o death is to set a just value on life.' *(William Hazlitt, 1778-1830)*

(His last words, incidentally, were: 'I have led a happy life.')

Democracy

'Vox populi, vox dei.' (The voice of the people is the voice o God.) *(Alcuin 735-804)*

'In all forms of Government the people is the true legislator. *(Edmund Burke, 1728-1797)*

Despair

'The mass of men lead lives of quiet desperation.' *(H. D Thoreau. 1817-1862)*

Diplomacy

'An ambassador is an honest man sent to lie abroad for his country.' *(Sir Henry Wotton, 1568-1639)*

Drinking

'There is nothing which has yet been contrived by man by which so much happiness is produced as by a good tavern.' *(Dr Johnson, 1709-1784)*

But elsewhere the Great Lexicographer added this warning:
'Melancholy, indeed, should be diverted by every means but drinking.'

Eating
Dr Johnson also had a comment to make on eating: 'I look upon it that he who does not mind his belly will hardly mind anything else.'

Education
'Reading is to the mind what exercise is to the body.' *(Richard Steele, 1671-1729)*

'A little learning is a dang'rous thing.' *(Alexander Pope, 1688-1744)*

Empire
'His Majesty's dominions, on which the sun never sets.' *(Christopher North, 1785-1854)*

Equality
'His lordship may compel us to be equal upstairs, but there will never be equality in the servants' hall.' *(J. M. Barrie, 1860-1937)*

Euthanasia

'Thou shalt not kill; but need'st not strive
Officiously to keep alive.'
(A. H. Clough, 1819-1861)

(The quotation, much bandied during discussions on euthanasia, comes from his poem *The Latest Decalogue,* a witty updating of the Ten Commandments.)

Evil
'The only thing necessary for the triumph of evil is for good men to do nothing.' *(Edmund Burke, 1729-1797)*

'The evil that men do lives after them,
The good is oft interred with their bones.'
(William Shakespeare, 1564-1616)

Faith
'Faith must trample underfoot all reason, sense and understanding.' *(Martin Luther, 1483-1546)*

Fame
'If fame is to come only after death, I'm in no hurry for it.' *(Martial, 40-102)*

And on the same theme:

'Fame is a food that dead men eat—
I have no stomach for such meat.'
(Henry Austin Dobson, 1840-1921)

Fanaticism
'The worst vice of the fanatic is his sincerity.' *(Oscar Wilde, 1856-1900)*

Fatalism
'Things and actions are what they are, and the consequences of them will be what they will be: why then should we desire to be deceived?' *(Joseph Butler, 1692-1752)*

Folly

'How pleasant it is, at the end of the day,
No follies to have to repent,
But reflect on the past, and be able to say,
That my time has been properly spent.'
(Jane Taylor, 1783-1827)

Food
'Imprisoned in every fat man, a thin one is wildly signalling to be let out.' *(Cyril Connolly, 1903-1974)*

Freedom
'None can love freedom heartily, but good men; the rest love not freedom, but licence.' *(John Milton, 1608-1674)*

'Necessity is the plea for every infringement of human freedom. It is the argument of tyrants; it is the creed of slaves.' *(William Pitt, 1759-1806)*

Generosity
'He gives twice who gives quickly.' *(Attr. to Publilius Syrus, fl. 1st century BC)*

'Rich gifts wax poor when givers prove unkind.'
(William Shakespeare, 1564-1616)

Genius
'In the republic of mediocrity, genius is dangerous.' *(Robert G. Ingersoll, 1833-1899)*

'Genius does what it must, and Talent does what it can. *(Earl of Lytton, 1831-1891)*

Government
'If the State acts in ways abhorrent to human nature, it is the lesser evil to destroy it.' *(Baruch Spinoza, 1632-1677)*

Greatness
'Great men are the guide-posts and landmarks in the state.' (Edmund Burke, 1728-1797)

'No greater proof can be given by a man of his own littleness than disbelief in great men.' *(Edmund Burke)*

'The world's great men have not commonly been great scholars, nor its great scholars great men.' *(Oliver Wendell Holmes, 1809-1894)*

Habit
'The second half of a man's life is made up of nothing but the habits he has acquired during the first half.' *(Feodor Dostoievsky, 1821-1881)*

Happiness
'All happy families resemble each other; each unhappy family is unhappy in its own way.' *(Leo Tolstoy, 1828-1910)*

'A lifetime of happiness: no man alive could bear it; it would be hell on earth.' *(G. B. Shaw, 1856-1950)*

'It is a flaw
In happiness, to see beyond our bourn –
It forces us in summer skies to mourn,
It spoils the singing of the nightingale.'
(John Keats, 1795-1821)

'Travelling is the ruin of all happiness! There's no looking at a building here after seeing Italy.' *(Fanny Burney, 1752-1840)*

'Not in Utopia – subterranean fields –
Or some secreted island, Heaven knows where!
But in the very world, which is the world
Of all of us – the place where, in the end
We find our happiness, or not at all!'
(William Wordsworth, 1770-1850)

'Ask yourself whether you are happy, and you cease to be so.' *(J. S. Mill, 1806-1873)*

'Happy the man, and happy he alone,
He, who can call today his own:
He who, secure within, can say,
Tomorrow do thy worst, for I have lived today.'
(John Dryden, 1631-1701)

'No one can be perfectly happy till all are happy.' *(Herbert Spencer, 1820-1903)*

Heresy
'It is the customary fate of new truths to begin as heresies and to end as superstitions.' *(T. H. Huxley, 1825-1895)*

'Heresy signifies no more than private opinion.' *(Thomas Hobbes, 1588-1679)*

'How can what an Englishman believes be heresy? It is a contradiction in terms.' *(G. B. Shaw, 1856-1950)*

Heroism
'Nothing of what is nobly done can ever be lost.' *(Charles Dickens, 1812-1870)*

(Dickens's friend and first biographer, John Forster, records that the novelist was particularly affected by silent heroisms.)

History
'Assassination has never changed the history of the world.' *(Benjamin Disraeli, 1804-1881).*
(But then, he lived before the assassination of the Archduke Ferdinand at Sarajevo, which sparked off World War One!)

'Ideas shape the course of history.' *(J. M. Keynes, 1883-1946)*

'History is a set of lies agreed upon.' *(Napoleon Bonaparte, 1769-1821)*

'History is only a confused heap of facts.' *(Earl of Chesterfield, 1694-1773)*

Hope
'Hope is generally a wrong guide, though it is very good company by the way.' *(George Savile, Marquis of Halifax, 1633-1695)*

Humility
'I have never met a man so ignorant I could not learn something from him.' *(Galileo, 1564-1642)*

Idealism
'Idealism increases in direct proportion to one's distance from the problem.' *(John Galsworthy, 1867-1933)*

Idleness
'Idleness is only the refuge of weak minds.' *(Earl of Chesterfield, 1694-1773)*

Integrity
'He that toucheth pitch shall be defiled therewith.' *(Apocrypha)*
'In times when a government imprisons any unjustly, the true

place for a just man is also the prison.' *(H. D. Thoreau, 1817-1862)*

Insult
'An injury is much sooner forgotten than an insult.' *(Earl of Chesterfield, 1694-1773)*

Journalism
'Journalists say a thing that they know isn't true, in the hope that if they keep on saying it long enough it *will* be true.' *(Arnold Bennett, 1867-1931)*

Justice
'Justice is truth in action.' *(Benjamin Disraeli, 1804-1881)*

'Justice must tame, whom mercy cannot win.' *(George Savile, Marquis of Halifax, 1633-1695)*

Knowledge
'What man knows is everywhere at war with what he wants.' *(Joseph W. Krutch, b.1893)*

'They know enough who know how to learn.' *(Henry Adams, 1838-1918)*

Labour
'To travel hopefully is a better thing than to arrive, and the true success is to labour.' *(R. L. Stevenson, 1850-1894)*

Law
'Laws are like cobwebs, which may catch small flies, but let wasps and hornets break through.' *(Jonathan Swift, 1667-1745)*

'How long soever it hath continued, if it be against reason, it is of no force in law.' *(Sir Edward Coke, 1552-1634)*

'The law is a ass – a idiot.' *(The Parochial Beadle, Bumble, in Dickens's novel Oliver Twist)*

Learning

'He was wont to say that if he had read as much as other men, he should have known no more than other men.' *(John Aubrey, 1626-1697, on Hobbes)*

'It is better to be able neither to read nor write than to be able to do nothing else.' *(William Hazlitt, 1778-1830)*

Liberty

'A nation may lose its liberties in a day and not miss them in a century.' *(Baron de Montesquieu, 1689-1755)*

Life

'God and the doctor we alike adore
But only when in danger, not before;
The danger o'er, both are alike requited,
God is forgotten, and the Doctor slighted.'
(John Owen, c.1560-1622)

'Sic transit gloria mundi.' (So passes the glory of the world.) *(Thomas à Kempis, 1380-1471)*

'Life is not living, but living well.' *(Martial, 43-120)*

'If you would be known, and not know, vegetate in a village; if you would know, and not be known, live in a city.' *(Charles Caleb Colton, c.1780-1832)*

'To live is like to love – all reason is against it, and all healthy instinct is for it.' *(Samuel Butler, 1835-1902)*

'Life is mostly froth and bubble,
Two things stand like stone,
Kindness in another's trouble,
Courage in your own.'
(Adam Lindsay Gordon, 1833-1870)

'Life's but a walking shadow, a poor player,
That struts and frets his hour upon the stage,
And then is heard no more; it is a tale

Told by an idiot, full of sound and fury,
Signifying nothing.'
(William Shakespeare, 1564-1616)

Love

'Love is like the measles; we all have to go through it.' *(Jerome K. Jerome, 1859-1927)*

'Love warps the mind a little from the right.' *(George Crabbe, 1754-1832)*

'Love is not love
Which alters when it alteration finds.'
(William Shakespeare, 1564-1616)

Maxims

'Honesty is the best policy; but he who is governed by that maxim is not an honest man.' *(Richard Whately, 1787-1863)*

'Laugh, and the world laughs with you;
Weep, and you weep alone.'
(Ella Wheeler Wilcox, 1855-1919)

'Silence is the virtue of fools.' *(Francis Bacon, 1561-1626)*

'We have all enough strength to bear the misfortune of others.' *(La Rochefoucauld, 1613-1680)*

'The height of cleverness is to be able to conceal it.' *(La Rochefoucauld, 1613-1680)*

Man

'Homo sum; humani nil a me alienum puto.' (I am a man; I count nothing human indifferent to me.) *(Terence, c.190-159 BC)*

'Man is distinguished from all other creatures by the faculty of laughter.' *(Joseph Addison, 1672-1719)*

'It is human nature to think wisely and act foolishly.' *(Anatole France, 1844-1924)*

Memories

'There is no greater sorrow than to recall, in misery, the time when we were happy.' *(Dante, 1265-1321)*

Merit

'It is better to deserve honours and not have them than to have them and not deserve them.' *(Mark Twain, 1835-1910)*

Money

'Who goeth a borrowing
Goeth a sorrowing.'
(Thomas Tusser, c.1524-1580)

'Let us all be happy, and live within our means, even if we have to borrow the money to do it with.' *(Artemus Ward, 1834-1867)*

'Be not a beggar by banqueting upon borrowing.' *(Apocrypha)*

'Annual income twenty pounds, annual expenditure nineteen, nineteen six, result happiness. Annual income twenty pounds, annual expenditure twenty pounds and six, result misery.' *(Micawber in Dickens's novel David Copperfield)*

'Pity the poor millionaire, for the way of the philanthropist is hard.' *(Andrew Carnegie, 1835-1919)*

'Money cures melancholy.' *(John Ray, 1628-1705)*

Morality

'We know no spectacle so ridiculous as the British public in one of its periodic fits of morality.' *(Lord Macaulay, 1800-1859)*

Music

Sir Jack Westrup, commenting on the versatility of Henry Purcell (c.1658-1695), wrote: 'He could bid the trumpets to sound for majesty, or seeking flight from love's sickness find the fever in himself.'

Beethoven (1770-1827) on Handel: 'He was the greatest composer that ever lived. I would uncover my head, and kneel before his tomb.' Handel lived from 1685 to 1759.

Edward Elgar (1857-1934), writing in 1900 on the frustration of not being able to hear his work being performed because, like other prophets, he had no honour in his land, wrote: 'I always said God was against art and I still believe it. Anything obscene or trivial is blessed in this world and has a reward. I ask for no reward – only to live and hear my work.' (Happily, he did.)

Now, some quotations on or from some modern popular composers. Richard Rodgers, contemporary composer of *Oklahoma, The Sound of Music,* etc., was asked, 'Which comes first – the words or the music?' He replied: 'The cheque.'

Of Cole Porter (1893-1964), Richard Adler remarked: 'He was the Adlai Stevenson of songwriters . . . he was an aristocrat in everything he did and everything he wrote. Everything had class – even a little pop song like *Don't fence me in . . .'*

Oscar Levant (1906-1972), pianist and drinker, wrote in his *Memoirs of an Amnesiac,* 'My behaviour has been impeccable; I've been unconscious for the past six months.'

Alexander Woolcott, the famous critic, said of Levant, 'There is nothing wrong with Oscar that a miracle cannot cure.'

Levant, in his Memoirs, quotes George Gershwin, on hearing that a girl he had loved had since married: 'If I wasn't so busy, I'd be upset.'

And a final one from Levant. Poking fun at Gershwin, who was undergoing psychoanalysis, he asked, 'Does it help your constipation, George?' Gershwin replied, 'No, but now I understand why I have constipation.'

New World

'The next Augustan age will dawn on the other side of the Atlantic. There will, perhaps, be a Thucydides at Boston, a Xenophon at New York, and, in time, a Virgil at Mexico, and a Newton at Peru. At last, some curious traveller from Lima will visit England and give a description of the ruins of St Paul's . . .' *(Horace Walpole, 1717-1797)*

Opinion
'Nothing is more unjust or capricous than public opinion.' *(William Hazlitt, 1778-1830)*

'We are all of us more or less the slaves of opinion.' *(William Hazlitt)*

'That man is best who considers everything for himself.' *(Hesiod, c.35 BC)*

Opportunity
'A wise man will make more opportunities than he finds.' *(Francis Bacon, 1561-1626)*

'When one door is shut, another opens.' *(Cervantes, 1547-1616)*

Patriotism
'It is a fine and honourable thing to die for one's country.' ('Dulce et decorum est pro patria mori.') *(Horace, 65-8BC)*

'I realise that patriotism is not enough. I must have no hatred or bitterness towards any one.' *(Edith Cavell, 1865-1915)*
(These were her last words before she was shot by the Germans on October 12, 1915, for spying.)

'No man can be a patriot on an empty stomach.' *(William Cowper, 1731-1800)*

Philosophy
'Irrationally held truths may be more harmful than reasoned errors.' *(T. H. Huxley, 1825-1895)*

'Two men look out through the same bars;
One sees the mud, and one the stars.'
(Frederick Langbridge, 1849-1923)

'Opinion is ultimately determined by the feelings, and not by the intellect.' *(Herbert Spencer, 1820-1903)*

'Happy is he who can recognise the causes of things.' *(Virgil, 70-19 BC)*

'In every parting there is an image of death.' *(George Eliot, 1819-1880)*

Poetry
'As civilisation advances, poetry almost necessarily declines.' *(Lord Macaulay, 1800-1859)*

'All poets are mad.' *(Robert Burton, 1577-1640)*

'Poets are the unacknowledged legislators of the world.' *(Percy Bysshe Shelley, 1792-1822)*

'God is the perfect poet
Who in his person acts his own creations.'
(Robert Browning, 1812-1889)

Politics
'You can fool all the people some of the time, and some of the people all the time, but you can not fool all the people all of the time.' *(Abraham Lincoln, 1809-1865)*

'The well-being of the people is the supreme law.' *(Cicero, 106-43 BC)*

'I seldom think of politics more than eighteen hours a day.' *(Lyndon B. Johnson, 1908-1973)*

'I never believed in frontal attacks either in war or politics if there was a way round.' *(Lloyd George, 1863-1945)*

'There is a holy mistaken zeal in politics as well as in religion. By persuading others, we convince ourselves.' *(Junius, fl.1770)*
(This was the pseudonym of a Whig satirist, possibly Sir Philip Francis, 1740-1818.)

Politicians
On Chamberlain (1869-1940), Lloyd George is credited with

remarking: 'He saw foreign policy through the wrong end of a municipal drainpipe.'

On Asquith (1852-1928), Lady Cunard commented, 'Black and wicked and with only a nodding acquaintance with the truth.'

Power
'A man may build himself a throne of bayonets, but he cannot sit on it.' *(Dean Inge, 1864-1954)*

'The greater the power, the greater the abuse.' *(Edmund Burke, 1728-1797)*
(The same dictum was expressed slightly differently in more recent times by Lord Acton: 'All power tends to corrupt; absolute power corrupts absolutely.')

Burke also had this to say on the subject: 'Those who have been once intoxicated with power, and have derived any kind of emolument from it, even though but for one year, can never willingly abandon it.'

Progress
'All that is human must retrograde if it does not advance.' *(Edward Gibbon, 1737-1794)*

Proverbs
'Thieves hunt in couples but a liar alone.' *(American)*

'He that can make a fire well can end a quarrel.' *(English)*

'There is but an hour a day between a good housewife and a bad one.' *(English)*

'When the husband drinks to the wife, all would be well; when the wife drinks to the husband, all is.' *(English)*

'Courage ought to have eyes as well as arms.' *(English)*

'What is said when drunk has been thought out beforehand.' *(Flemish)*

'He who fondles you more than usual has either deceived you or wants to do so.' *(French)*

'He who can lick can bite.' *(French)*

'Street angel, house devil.' *(German)*

'Better be quarrelling than lonesome.' *(Irish)*

'Money swore on oath that nobody that did not love it should ever have it.' *(Irish)*

'When a man say him do not mind, then him mind.' *(Negro)*

'That which everybody guards will soon disappear.' *(Polish)*

'Even were a cook to cook a fly, he would keep the breast for himself.' *(Polish)*

'Visits always give pleasure – if not the arrival, the departure.' *(Portuguese)*

'To change one's habits has a smell of death.' *(Portuguese)*

'The devil's boots don't creak.' *(Scottish)*

'Only God helps the badly dressed.' *(Spanish)*

'To tell a woman what she may not do is to tell her what she can.' *(Spanish)*

'The afternoon knows what the morning never suspected.' *(Swedish)*

'A good spectator also creates.' *(Swiss)*

'The priest's friend loses his faith, the doctor's his health, the lawyer's his fortune.' *(Venetian)*

'One good deed has many claimants.' *(Yiddish)*

'A fool is his own informer.' *(Yiddish)*

'If God lived on earth, people would break his windows.' *(Yiddish)*

'God will provide – ah, if only He would till He does so!' *(Yiddish)*

'A man too good for the world is no good for his wife.' *(Yiddish)*

Progress
'All progress is based upon a universal desire on the part of every organism to live beyond its means.' *(Samuel Butler, 1835-1902)*

'The reasonable man adapts himself to the world: the unreasonable one persists in trying to adapt the world to himself. Therefore all progress depends on the unreasonable man.' *(G. B. Shaw, 1856-1950)*

Prudence
'Prudence is a rich, old maid courted by incapacity.' *(William Blake, 1757-1827)*

Public Schools
'There is now less flogging in our great schools than formerly, but less is learned there: so what the boys get at one end they lose at the other.' *(Dr Johnson, 1709-1784)*

Quiet
'Anythin' for a quiet life (as the man said when he took the situation at the lighthouse).' *(Sam Weller in Dickens's novel Pickwick Papers)*

Reflection
'When a man knows he is to be hanged in a fortnight, it concentrates his mind wonderfully.' *(Dr Johnson, 1709-1784)*

Religion
'A God all mercy is a God unjust.' *(Edward Young, 1683-1765)*

'Scratch the Christian and you find the pagan – spoiled.' *(Israel Zangwill, 1864-1926)*

'What is a man profited, if he shall gain the whole world, and lose his own soul?' *(St Matthew)*

'Be a sinner and sin strongly, but more strongly have faith and rejoice in Christ.' *(Martin Luther, 1483-1546)*

'Our humanity were a poor thing were it not for the divinity which stirs within us.' *(Francis Bacon, 1561-1626)*

'Ten thousand difficulties do not make one doubt.' *(Cardinal Newman, 1801-1890)*

'The English Bible, a book which, if everything else in our language should perish, would alone suffice to show the whole extent of its beauty and power.' *(Lord Macaulay, 1800-1859)*

'Superstition is the religion of feeble minds.' *(Edmund Burke, 1728-1797)*

Self-love

'We sometimes imagine we hate flattery, but we only hate the way we are flattered.' *(La Rochefoucauld, 1613-1680)*

Smoking

'Herein is not only a great vanity, but a great contempt of God's good gifts, that the sweetness of man's breath, being a good gift of God, should be wilfully corrupted by this stinking smoke.' *(James I and VI, 1566-1625)*

'For thy sake, Tobacco, I
Would do anything but die.'
(Charles Lamb, 1775-1834)

'No woman should marry a teetotaller, or a man who does not smoke.' *(R. L. Stevenson, 1850-1894)*

'Pernicious weed! whose scent the fair annoys,
Unfriendly to society's chief joys,

Thy worst effect is banishing for hours
The sex whose presence civilises ours.'
(William Cowper, 1731-1800)

Stupidity
'With stupidity the gods themselves struggle in vain.' *(Friedrich von Schiller, 1759-1805)*

Style
'People think I can teach them style. What stuff it is! Have something to say and say it as clearly as you can. That is the only secret of style.' *(Matthew Arnold, 1822-1888)*
On the same theme, George Bernard Shaw (1856-1950) wrote: 'He who has nothing to assert has no style and can have none.'

Thinking
'Reading is sometimes an ingenious device for avoiding thought.' *(William Hazlitt, 1778-1830)*
'It's dogged as does it. It ain't thinking about it.' *(Anthony Trollope, 1815-1882)*

'We were to do more business after dinner; but after dinner is after dinner – an old saying and a true, "much drinking, little thinking".' *(Jonathan Swift, 1667-1745)*

'Plain living and high thinking are no more.' *(William Wordsworth, 1770-1850)*

'There is nothing either good or bad, but thinking makes it so.' *(William Shakespeare, 1564-1616)*

'They always talk, who never think.' *(Matthew Prior, 1664-1721)*

'The world is a comedy to those that think, a tragedy to those that feel.' *(Horace Walpole, 1717-1797)*

Tolerance
'No man can justly censure or condemn another, because indeed no man truly knows another.' *(Sir Thomas Browne, 1605-1682)*

'Tolerance is a two-edged sword.' *(J. Fenn, b.1947)*

Truth
'A big lie is more plausible than truth.' *(Ernest Hemingway, 1898-1961)*

'Few enthusiasts can be trusted to speak the truth.' *(A. J. Balfour, 1848-1930)*

'Whispering tongues can poison truth.' *(Samuel Taylor Coleridge, 1772-1834)*

'Truth be veiled, but still it burneth.' *(Percy Bysshe Shelley, 1792-1822)*

'Tis strange – but true; for truth is always strange; Stranger than fiction.' *(Lord Byron, 1788-1824)*

Unity
'Qui unum tangit omnes tangit.' (Who touches one touches all.) *(Anon.)*
(This is the motto of the London Retail Meat Traders.)

Vice
'We make a ladder of our vices, if we trample those same vices underfoot.' *(St Augustine, 354-430)*

War
'Force, and fraud, are in war the two cardinal virtues.' *(Thomas Hobbes, 1588-1679)*

'What is our task? To make Britain a fit country for heroes to live in.' *(Lloyd George, 1863-1945)*

'I used to say of him (Napoleon) that his presence on the field made the difference of 40,000 men.' *(Duke of Wellington, 1769-1852)*

'The world must be made safe for democracy.' *(Woodrow Wilson, addressing Congress on April 2, 1917)*

'But what can war but endless war still breed?.' *(John Milton, 1608-1674)*

Wit

'A sharp tongue is the only edged tool that grows keener with constant use.' *(Washington Irving, 1783-1859)*

'Man is a creature who lives not upon bread alone, but principally by catchwords.' *(R. L. Stevenson, 1850-1894)*

Woman

'A woman's whole life is a history of the affections.' *(Washington Irving, 1783-1859)*

Weather

'Ill is the weather that bringeth no gain.' *(Thomas Dekker, c.1570-1632)*

Youth

'The days of our youth are the days of our glory.' *(Lord Byron, 1788-1824)*

Zeal

'Pas trop de zele,' (Not too much enthusiasm). *(de Talleyrand, 1754-1834)*

Folksy

As a footnote to these quotations, here's a folk saying which is rather different – not because it is any less accurate but because its interpretation is disputed:

Ne'er cast a clout
Till May is out.

The obvious meaning is that you shouldn't discard items of winter clothing until the end of May. However, there is a school of thought which reckons that 'May' is the hawthorn blossom which flowers early in the month.

And in recent days, a really bizarre theory has been put forward (possibly 'tongue in cheek'). It is that the May in question was May Dennison, one of the 'fourpenny drabs' sleeping out around the 'Itchy Park' area of London's Shoreditch in the 1840s. This old soak, not caring much for winter weather, contrived to spend that period of the year in jail, emerging at the end of May. Hence the jeer of contemporary harlots about not casting a clout.

We reckon that theory won't hold water. For a start, the saying is a good deal older than the 1840s, and a good deal more widespread than London, being quoted in the north of England and Scotland among other places. And for that matter, the constabulary are hardly likely to have been so accommodating to a scabrous whore!

That leaves the other two theories, and there is no doubt the meaning 'don't discard clothing till the end of May' is the right one. This is how it was understood by the folks of old. For example, this version of the rhyme is found in Cheshire:

'Don put off your winter clothes
Till you see the June rose.'

And this meaning is confirmed by another saying that a May cold lasts thirty days.

Getting it wrong

In the first volume of excerpts from our LBB we included a section of celebrated misquotations. Here, to conclude this chapter, is a handful of others to supplement them, boobs connected with Show-biz.

Everybody knows that in the film *Casablanca* Humphrey Bogart says, 'Play it again, Sam.' Or did he? Answer, 'no'. What Bogey said was, 'You know what I want to hear – you played it for her (Ingrid Bergman), you can play it for me. If she can stand it, I can. Play it!' The words, 'Play it again, Sam', were actually spoken by Anne Baxter in another film, *The Spoilers*.

Lonely heart

And what of Greta Garbo? In the film *Grand Hotel* she is supposed to have turned to John Barrymore and said, 'I want to be alone.' Almost. In fact, she said, 'I want to be left alone.'

Other non-sayings which have hit the history books as authentic are: (a) Charles Boyer's 'Come weez me to zee Casbah' which never hit the sound track of the 1938 film, *Algiers*; (b) Johnny Weismuller's 'Me Tarzan, you Jane';